Building Web Applications with Erlang

Zachary Kessin

O'REILLY®

Beijing · Cambridge · Farnham · Köln · Sebastopol · Tokyo

Building Web Applications with Erlang
by Zachary Kessin

Published by O'Reilly Media, Inc., 1005 Gravenstein Highway North, Sebastopol, CA 95472.

O'Reilly books may be purchased for educational, business, or sales promotional use. Online editions are also available for most titles (*http://my.safaribooksonline.com*). For more information, contact our corporate/institutional sales department: 800-998-9938 or *corporate@oreilly.com*.

Editor: Simon St. Laurent	**Cover Designer:** Karen Montgomery
Production Editor: Melanie Yarbrough	**Interior Designer:** David Futato
Proofreader: Emily Quill	**Illustrator:** Robert Romano

Revision History for the First Edition:
   2012-06-04   First release
See *http://oreilly.com/catalog/errata.csp?isbn=9781449309961* for release details.

ISBN: 978-1-449-30996-1

[LSI]

1338839909

Table of Contents

Preface

Erlang promises to let you build robust, fault-tolerant servers far more easily than with Java or C#. It almost sounds too good to be true, but Erlang has become a programmer's secret handshake. As much as many of us hate our phone company, there is a basic truth that must be recognized: when you pick up your phone to make a call, it normally just works. So people have started to realize that telecom folks must be doing something right!

Erlang was built to program telephone switches at Ericsson, and most of the language design choices reflect what was necessary to program a telephone switch. That means, for example, that Erlang software can run for years at a time without interruption because phone switches are expected to do that. Erlang applications can be upgraded in place without taking the system offline or even losing state because the phone company can't drop a city's worth of calls every time they have to patch a bug or roll out a new feature.

When a web service goes down, a lot of things break. It may not be as obvious as a suddenly interrupted call, but it may actually create more problems as failures create new failures. Web services can benefit from the language design decisions Erlang's creators made in a telephone switching environment. Having a server that can run without interruption can allow a development team to provide a better service to their customers.

Who This Book Is For

This book shows you the baby steps to building a web service with Erlang. It does not try to teach you Erlang (there are other books for that), nor does it try to show you how to build the large-scale applications that really call for Erlang. Instead, it shows you how to build simple web services as a step along the way to learning to build large-scale web services.

I expect that many readers will, like me, be long-time web professionals who are looking at Erlang as a way to stand out from a crowd of Java and C# developers. After all, in a few years Erlang may be the next big thing, and you want to be ahead of the wave. Or perhaps you have become frustrated with some aspect of building web applications in those other languages and are looking for something a bit more powerful.

You need to know at least basic Erlang, but you should also be familiar with web development—in PHP, Perl, Ruby, Java, or something else. I assume that you have seen HTML and know the basics of how HTTP works.

There are a few examples in this book that use JavaScript to interface a browser with the Erlang example. Except in Chapter 9, this code is not critical to understanding what the Erlang code is doing, although of course if you are building a large web application it will contain JavaScript. I also use CoffeeScript in a few places. CoffeeScript is a small language that compiles down to JavaScript and generally makes for a much nicer programming experience than straight JavaScript.[1]

Learning Erlang

This book will not teach you Erlang. There are already a number of good resources for that, including:

- *Learn You Some Erlang for Great Good* (*http://learnyousomeerlang.com*), by Fred Hébert. *Learn You Some Erlang* will also be published by No Starch Press in September 2012.
- *Erlang Programming*, by Francesco Cesarini and Simon Thompson, published by O'Reilly.
- *Programming Erlang*, by Joe Armstrong, published by The Pragmatic Programmers.

Reading the first few chapters of any of these and understanding the basics of how Erlang works should be enough. However, you should plan to really work through those chapters and write some simple programs before attempting the projects here.

In particular, you should read up on sequential code and the very basics of how concurrency works in Erlang. When building large-scale applications in Erlang, taking advantage of the Open Telecom Platform (OTP) will allow the programmer to leverage a large amount of well-tested functionality. And while OTP is very powerful and will make development in Erlang much easier, the details of OTP are less important to learn up front and can be learned as you go along after you have an understanding of how other parts of the system work.

---

1. You can find more information about CoffeeScript at *http://coffeescript.org*.

Before You Start

Before you dive into this book, you should have Erlang and Yaws installed on your system. (If you need help in this, check Appendix A.) Erlang and Yaws can be run on Windows, Mac, and Linux, so any type of system will work fine.

 Several people have asked me why I wrote this book around Yaws and not some other web package. There were a few reasons. First of all, Yaws seemed the easiest package to get something simple working in. Second, several of the other packages do not support web sockets (or at least didn't when I started writing), and I knew that I would be needing web sockets in my own development.

I am also assuming that you are familiar with the Unix command line. While it is not necessary to be a Bash Kung-Fu Master (I'm not), you should be able to interact with the bash shell and not freak out.

What You Will Learn

Building a full Erlang application requires a large set of skills. This book will help you get to the point where you can build a basic web service application and get it running.

First, you'll explore some of the power and mystery of Erlang and REST. You'll see why Erlang makes sense as a foundation for building scalable and reliable systems and why REST is a popular approach to building web services and explore some of the tradeoffs involved in using the two together. This first chapter will also explore some of your data storage options.

The Yaws web server is the foundation of our application, so you'll learn to configure Yaws and serve static content. Yes, static content. In many cases, a website with dynamic content will have a collection of static files as resources. Once you know how to manage static files, you can move on to working with dynamic content, embedding Erlang into an HTML file or other kind of file (see "Dynamic Content in Yaws" on page 21). You'll learn about working with HTTP itself and basic debugging tools like logging.

You'll need a way to route client requests presented as URLs to the internal resources of your service. Appmods, discussed in Chapter 3, will let you map arbitrary URLs onto relevant resources.

Next we cover output formats. I will show three general ways to output data to the user. The first, and least useful, method is to use ehtml to directly translate Erlang data into HTML or XML. We also will see how to use the erlydtl library to use the Django template language to create formatted output. (DTL is a common template package on Python and should be familiar to some readers of this book.) Finally, we will see how to encode Erlang data structures into JSON or XML, which can be sent to the user. In many cases, modern web applications will have a page of static (or almost static) HTML and a lot of JavaScript that will interact with the server by sending JSON or XML over Ajax channels.

Now that we can generate content, it's time to build a simple RESTful service. You'll assemble an application that can listen for HTTP requests, process them, store data, and return useful information. You'll also learn how to handle large chunks of incoming information, dealing with multipart requests and file uploads.

If you'd like to go beyond HTTP's request-response model, Chapter 6 presents a live bidirectional method of communication between the client and the server. Yaws supports web sockets, and the dynamic, event-driven nature of Erlang makes for an ideal platform for pushing dynamic data to the client.

Finally, Chapter 9 presents a somewhat larger example that pulls together most or all of the previously discussed topics into one complete application. This chapter will show how to build a complete small application with Yaws and OTP.

The Limits of This Book

If you want a complete guide to building large, fault-tolerant sites with Erlang, you'll be disappointed. The architecture of a large-scale website requires a book of its own. (A project like that will probably end up being 90% backend and logic and 10% web interface.)

I also deliberately did not cover any of the half dozen or so frameworks for building web applications with Erlang, as I wanted to focus on the task of building a basic service in Erlang with just Yaws and custom code. MochiWeb, Chicago Boss, Nitrogen, Zotonic, and the rest need their own books, but I summarize them briefly in Appendix B.

This book does not attempt to show how to structure an Erlang application beyond the very basics: a full introduction to OTP requires a longer book than this one.

It is also not an introduction to supervision trees. They are covered briefly in Chapter 9, but this is a short introduction to a very large topic.

Erlang has a full set of features to allow it to monitor the state of an application and respond when processes or nodes go offline. This is amazingly powerful on many levels. For example, in the case of a node failing at 2:00 AM, Erlang can generate a log message and create a new node from a cloud with no need for human intervention—a far better scenario than an emergency wake up call for the sysadmin!

For automated testing, Erlang has a test framework called EUnit (documented in *Erlang Programming*) as well as a version of the Haskell QuickCheck testing suite. These are beyond the scope of this book, but can be quite useful for development.

Finally, this book does not cover details of how best to run Erlang on Amazon EC2 or other cloud services. Running a bunch of Erlang nodes on cloud hosts can make a lot of sense.

Help! It Doesn't Compile or Run!

When working with a new framework in a language you may not know very well, it is inevitable that sooner or later you will hit a few problems. Code won't compile, or else it will compile and then crash in all sorts of strange ways.

If you are anything like me, you probably won't be doing a copy/paste of code directly from this book (though you are welcome to do so if you want); instead, you'll probably try to adapt this code to some other problem you are trying to solve. After all, that's the whole point of books like this—to give you tools to solve problems in fun new ways. So what should you do if something doesn't work as expected?

Diagnosing the Error

If a request to Yaws docs not work, it will show a screen link, as shown in Figure P-1. This may look a bit cryptic at first glance, but is actually quite helpful. First of all, you will notice the path to the file that contains the Erlang module with the offending code. Then you will see the reason why it crashed (in this case, a call to a function in an unloaded module), and then the request that was made and the stack trace. In Erlang R15 this stack trace will also include line numbers; this screen shot is from R14B02, which does not include them.

Figure P-1. Error Page

What Version of Erlang and Yaws Are You Running?

This book was built around Erlang R14B02 and R15B. Ideally you should use R15B or later. This is a major release that among other features includes line numbers in stack traces, which makes finding errors much easier. You can find the version of Erlang you have by running `erl -v` from the command line.

This book was also built with Yaws version 1.92. You can find your version of Yaws by running `yaws -v` from the command line. The web sockets interface described in Chapter 6 changed in a major way between Yaws versions 1.90 and 1.92.

Is Everything Loaded Correctly?

Programmers who have come to Erlang from languages like PHP or Perl will find that there is an extra step in Erlang. While Yaws will automatically compile and load new `.yaws` files (see "Dynamic Content in Yaws" on page 21), any other Erlang module must be compiled and loaded into the Erlang runtime. Compilation can be done from within the Erlang shell by using the `c(Module).` command, which will also load the new code into the Erlang runtime. This is very useful for interactive testing of code and for the speed of your development cycle. It's certainly possible that someone converting from PHP to Erlang will forget this step from time to time.

Erlang code can also be compiled from an external command line with the `erlc` command from a Unix shell.[2] Erlang will autoload the code; however, it is important to set the include paths correctly so that it can find the *.beam* files. This option is good for doing things like automatic builds. The loading of external modules may be automated by adding the load commands to the *.erlang* file or other configuration options.

In addition, Erlang applications will often be composed of many modules, all of which must be loaded into the system for it to work. So if something fails, check to see if a module has not been loaded or is not in the path. To see the current path from the shell, run `code:get_path()`.

One nice thing about Erlang is that if the system is set up in a reasonable way, you should never need to take the entire system offline to upload a new version of code.

Are You Calling Everything Correctly?

The Erlang command line is your friend! This is a good place to try out your code and see if it works as expected. Don't be afraid to create test data at the command line and give your functions test inputs to make sure that they return the correct results.

---

2. This also works with Cygwin on Windows.

When you load a module, its records are not loaded into the shell. This has to be done explicitly with the `rr` command from the Erlang shell. You can also define a record with `rd` and remove a record with `rf`. To use these, type `help()` on the Erlang command line.

Is Mnesia Running with Correct Tables?

Mnesia, Erlang's built-in database, has to be started up and tables created for it to work. Before you start Mnesia you have to run the command `mnesia:create_schema/1`, which creates the basic database storage for Mnesia; then, to start Mnesia use the command `application:start(mnesia)`. If you are having trouble with Mnesia tables, you can use the table viewer by typing `tv:start()` at the Erlang command prompt.

Is the Example Just Plain Wrong?

Obviously, I've tried to ensure that all the code in this book runs smoothly the first time, but it's possible that an error crept through. You'll want to check the errata on this book's web page (see the How to Contact Us section at the end of the Preface), and download the sample code, which will be updated to fix any errors found after publication.

Conventions Used in This Book

The following typographical conventions are used in this book:

Italic
> Indicates new terms, URLs, email addresses, filenames, and file extensions.

`Constant width`
> Used for program listings, as well as within paragraphs to refer to program elements such as variable or function names, databases, data types, environment variables, statements, and keywords.

`Constant width bold`
> Shows commands or other text that should be typed literally by the user.

`Constant width italic`
> Shows text that should be replaced with user-supplied values or by values determined by context.

This icon signifies a tip, suggestion, or general note.

 This icon indicates a warning or caution.

Using Code Examples

This book is here to help you get your job done. In general, you may use the code in this book in your programs and documentation. You do not need to contact us for permission unless you're reproducing a significant portion of the code. For example, writing a program that uses several chunks of code from this book does not require permission. Selling or distributing a CD-ROM of examples from O'Reilly books does require permission. Answering a question by citing this book and quoting example code does not require permission. Incorporating a significant amount of example code from this book into your product's documentation does require permission.

We appreciate, but do not require, attribution. An attribution usually includes the title, author, publisher, and ISBN. For example: "*Building Web Applications with Erlang* by Zachary Kessin (O'Reilly). Copyright 2012 Zachary Kessin, 978-1-449-30996-1."

If you feel your use of code examples falls outside fair use or the permission given above, feel free to contact us at *permissions@oreilly.com*.

Safari® Books Online

 Safari Books Online (*www.safaribooksonline.com*) is an on-demand digital library that delivers expert content in both book and video form from the world's leading authors in technology and business.

Technology professionals, software developers, web designers, and business and creative professionals use Safari Books Online as their primary resource for research, problem solving, learning, and certification training.

Safari Books Online offers a range of product mixes and pricing programs for organizations, government agencies, and individuals. Subscribers have access to thousands of books, training videos, and prepublication manuscripts in one fully searchable database from publishers like O'Reilly Media, Prentice Hall Professional, Addison-Wesley Professional, Microsoft Press, Sams, Que, Peachpit Press, Focal Press, Cisco Press, John Wiley & Sons, Syngress, Morgan Kaufmann, IBM Redbooks, Packt, Adobe Press, FT Press, Apress, Manning, New Riders, McGraw-Hill, Jones & Bartlett, Course

Technology, and dozens more. For more information about Safari Books Online, please visit us online.

How to Contact Us

Please address comments and questions concerning this book to the publisher:

O'Reilly Media, Inc.
1005 Gravenstein Highway North
Sebastopol, CA 95472
800-998-9938 (in the United States or Canada)
707-829-0515 (international or local)
707-829-0104 (fax)

We have a web page for this book, where we list errata, examples, and any additional information. You can access this page at:

http://oreil.ly/build_webapps_erlang

To comment or ask technical questions about this book, send email to:

bookquestions@oreilly.com

For more information about our books, courses, conferences, and news, see our website at *http://www.oreilly.com*.

Find us on Facebook: *http://facebook.com/oreilly*

Follow us on Twitter: *http://twitter.com/oreillymedia*

Watch us on YouTube: *http://www.youtube.com/oreillymedia*

Acknowledgments

A book is a team effort, and I could not have written this book without a great team behind me. First of all, I must thank Simon St. Laurent for giving me the chance to write this book and supporting me through the process of putting it together.

I would also like to thank Reuven Lerner, who has helped me become a consultant and made it much more fun than it would have been otherwise.

I also need to thank my Technical Reviewers:

Fred Hébert is the person behind *Learn You Some Erlang for Great Good* (*http://lear nyousomeerlang.com*), which is a great way to learn Erlang. You can find Fred on Twitter at @mononcqc.

Steve Vinoski has been a contributor and committer on the Yaws project since 2008. He also writes the "Functional Web" column for IEEE Internet Computing, covering the application of functional programming languages and techniques for the development of web systems. Find his columns online at *http://steve.vinoski.net/*.

Francesco Cesarini is the coauthor of *Erlang Programming* and the CEO of Erlang Solutions.

I also want to thank all the various people who emailed and tweeted me about this book. I hope you find it useful! Please feel free to contact me on Twitter at @zkessin.

Of course I need to thank Joe Armstrong for creating Erlang, and "klacke" (Claes Wikstrom) for creating Yaws along with various other parts of the Erlang Ecosystem. Without them, this book would not exist.

Finally I need to thank my wife, Devora, who put up with me spending many more hours in front of the computer than she might have wished, and put up with a few sinks full of dirty dishes that I took longer to do than I probably should have.

CHAPTER 1

Building Scalable Systems with Erlang and REST

In the early days of the Web, building systems was simple. Take a Linux box, put Perl or PHP on it, add Apache and MySQL, and you were ready to go. Of course, this system was pretty limited. If you wanted to scale it past one or two servers it got real hard, real fast. It turns out that building scalable distributed applications is difficult, and the tools available to build them are often less than ideal.

Over the first decade of the 21st century, companies like Google, Amazon, eBay, and many others found that they needed to scale not to a few servers but to a few thousand servers, or even tens or hundreds of thousands or more. This requires a very different way of thinking about how to build a system, and dropping many of the patterns that had been used in the past for smaller systems.

One alternate recipe that offers scalability, resilience, and flexibility is to create your sites and applications using Erlang, with the frontend being defined by a variety of web services.

Why Erlang?

When I was getting ready to write this book I described the idea to several programmer friends. They all said, "I would never think of building a large-scale website in Erlang." It may seem daunting, but Erlang has features that fit large-scale web projects perfectly.

Ericsson originally created Erlang, a functional language based on Prolog, to run in telecom switches in the 1980s. Telecom switches must run without interruption for long periods of time, and this drove many of the choices that were made in Erlang. It was built to support systems that would have to be fault tolerant and able to be upgraded in place without downtime. As it turns out, these features are ideal not only for telephone switches, but also for business-critical web services.

One of the first major projects to use Erlang was the Ericsson AXD301 switch, which used about a million lines of Erlang code along with some device drivers and other low-level components that were written in C. The AXD301 switch has achieved an unprecedented level of reliability in the field—in some cases, it has achieved "nine 9s" reliability![1] The amount of time that the system could be expected to be offline could be measured in milliseconds per year. (This was for the entire network, not a single node.)

Clearly, most systems written in Erlang will not achieve that level of reliability. With careful design and testing, it's possible for a system to hit six 9s (about 30 seconds of downtime per year). However, reaching that is beyond the scope of this book, and requires a very careful study of risks that may cause the system to be unavailable and ensuring that no single failure (in particular, beyond your code) could cause that. For example, having three connections to the Internet with different ISPs is great, but if all three go through the same conduit it only takes one guy with a backhoe to cut all three wires and take a system offline.

Erlang applications can be upgraded in place. If an application is running on a cluster of servers and a bug is discovered in one module, there is no need to stop the system to upgrade to a new version of the software—Erlang provides a method to upgrade the code as it runs so that customers never need to be interrupted. This is a major advantage over a system where an application needs to be offline for an hour or more each time a new version of the software is rolled out, costing real money as customers are not able to use the system.

Erlang is also designed to support clusters of computers. In fact, to have a scalable and fault-tolerant system, it *must* run on more than one computer. As any given computer can fail, it is important that the system be able to deal with the case of a node in the cluster going offline and still providing services to the customers. How many nodes a system should run on is a complex issue, but it starts with the question "What is the probability of all the remaining nodes failing before I can bring a new node online?"

 If you Google "Erlang", you will see references to "Erlang-B" and "Erlang-C". These are measures of telephone capacity that are probably of great importance if you are building a call center, but have nothing to do with the programming language.

Erlang's Advantages

Erlang does many things differently. In most programming languages, concurrency is an afterthought. Each process in PHP, for example, runs independently and generally communicates with other PHP processes only via external resources like a database or memcached server. In Erlang, concurrency is built in from the very base of the system.

---

1. In practice, this often means "The system was more reliable than our way of measuring it."

Another difference is that Erlang is a compiled language. In PHP you can just edit a file and go to the web server, and it will be running the new version. In Erlang you need to compile the code and load it into the system, and while this is not difficult, it does represent an extra step.

Perhaps the strangest thing about Erlang for a new Erlang programmer is that all variables are single assignment. In Java terms, it's as if all variables are final. This takes some time to adapt to, but is in fact quite powerful in a language where concurrent processing is normal. If a variable can never be changed, then locks become almost an irrelevant detail. The other advantage is that a single assignment variable can only have its value assigned in one place, so if it has the wrong value then determining where that value came from becomes much easier: it must have been set at initial assignment.

Erlang features a message passing model for concurrency, so there is no shared state between threads—removing the need for a programmer to set locks in code. If you need shared state, you can do it via the Mnesia database (see "Mnesia" on page 11), Mnesia supports transactions and locks, providing in effect a form of software transactional memory (STM) shared memory.

Erlang's processes are a feature of the language, not the operating system. An Erlang process is much lighter in weight than a similar OS process. Processes in Erlang communicate with each other by sending messages, which generally has very low overhead, but can be heavy if a large amount of data is being copied between processes.

 Unless specified otherwise, "processes" in this book refer to Erlang processes, not OS processes. Erlang's processes are very lightweight and have very fast switching and startup times.

Lack of Types

Erlang has been criticized for its lack of a type system, and it's true that Erlang does not have static typing like Haskell does. Type systems give programmers a way to prove that the program is consistent in how it treats data. However, in a distributed system like Erlang, providing that kind of static consistency has some practical costs.

Erlang allows you to upgrade a system while keeping it running. However, by doing this, you create a system that is inconsistent. If types are changed in a version change (and it is reasonable to assume that most version changes will involve changing types), demanding static typing means that nodes running the old version cannot communicate with nodes running the new version—and the same with processes within the same node.

Imagine a case where there are just two nodes in a system, both running the same version of some software. This is a consistent system, where the consistency is one of type definition. However, when it comes time to upgrade the system, there will be a period of time when one node is running the new software and the other is running the old software. At this point you have an inconsistent system with regard to types.

At this point you have a few options. If you had built your system in Haskell, you would probably need to have a partition in which nodes running the old version of the software could not talk to those running the new version. You could also just take the system down for a short period of time while you did the upgrade, therefore sacrificing the availability of the system but ensuring that the system while running is never partitioned and never inconsistent.

There is no general perfect solution to this problem. Erlang was built to optimize for maximum availability, as choices were made to allow it to be inconsistent in some ways while still making services available. It may in fact be possible to solve this in Haskell, but thus far no one has done so. Erlang was built with the assumption that errors will happen and that the system should have methods of dealing with them on an ongoing basis. Haskell was built to minimize errors, period. Different priorities led to different designs.

OTP—For More Than Just Telecom!

The Open Telecom Platform (OTP) framework for building fault-tolerant applications ships with Erlang. By setting up software to run inside the OTP framework, applications can take advantage of OTP's built-in fault recovery and monitoring. OTP automates much of the concurrency of Erlang, but what really makes it shine is its ability to monitor a running application and keep it running.

Erlang code takes a "let it crash" approach, unlike the `try/catch` blocks in many other languages. Erlang figures that when something goes wrong, let it go wrong, and don't try to duct tape it back together in an unknown state. OTP will restart monitored processes that die. This also has the benefit that a process that is on a node that has died can be restarted elsewhere. (Obviously a node cannot fix itself if the server it is on has died.) If you want a system that can be fault tolerant and continue to provide your service, you want a framework that can deal with failure and simply work around it.

This book builds an application using OTP in Chapter 9; however, this is not a complete introduction to the subject as I cover only the elements that are needed to write this specific application. The books *Erlang Programming* and *Programming Erlang* both provide a more detailed introduction, while the book *Erlang and OTP in Action* goes into much greater detail on OTP.

Why Web Services? Why REST?

Years of work with the Web have made people comfortable with the idea that a specific URL is tied to a specific resource. For example, the URL *http://en.wikipedia.org/wiki/ Erlang_(programming_language)* is the Wikipedia page on Erlang. It is obvious in this case how the URL relates to the underlying resource. For a web page meant to be read by a person with a web browser, this is a useful representation.

Before REST surfaced, emerging from careful study of how and why HTTP succeeded, developers created a number of ways to send a remote procedure call over a network. When HTTP became the dominant mechanism for Internet communications, many of those same mechanisms were repurposed to run over HTTP. This made broad sense, as HTTP tools are common, but didn't always take advantage of HTTP's strengths.

Prior to REST, people tended to tunnel services over SOAP. However, SOAP does not make very good use of HTTP—it sends only XML messages back and forth over HTTP POST requests. It doesn't take advantage of caching proxies or other features of the HTTP infrastructure, beyond HTTP's frequent ability to go through a firewall.

REST takes much better advantage of HTTP, using HTTP's limited set of request verbs and living within the expectations for their processing. This forces an approach of working with a limited number of actions on an unlimited number of possible resources. It takes some getting used to, but it offers a consistent and powerful way to send information across networks that it easily integrated with web infrastructure and interfaces.

 For full details on how a REST service should work, take a look at *REST in Practice* by Webber, Parastatidis, and Robinson (*http://restinpractice .com*).

REST treats URLs—usually called Uniform Resource Identifiers (URIs) in this context —as the fundamental way to address an underlying resource. Furthermore, a resource may have several representations; so for example, an ebook may be accessible as a PDF, mobi, or some other format.

In a RESTful service, the four HTTP verbs GET, POST, PUT, and DELETE have well defined meanings. A GET request should only retrieve information. A GET should also be idempotent: a client can call it as many times as needed, and it will not change the state of the system in any way the client will care about. (For example, it may add information to logs, but not change user-facing data.) As long as the server sets an ETag or a Cache-Control header, this makes it easy for a proxy server or client to cache a resource, allowing much faster response on reads across a network. (HEAD and OPTIONS requests, if you use them, should also be idempotent.)

The POST method will create a new entity, which could be a chatroom or a record in a database. The PUT method will replace a resource with a new version. This can be used to update records or the like. The DELETE method is used to remove a resource.

REST defines the DELETE and PUT methods so that they are repeatable. That is to say, calling them several times will have the same effect on a system as calling them once.

For example, if you call DELETE on a resource one time or four, it should still have the end result that the resource is deleted (or an error is generated).

In a RESTful service the URL should reliably serve to identify the resource to be worked on. In many ways, you'll want to build by identifying your resources first, and then figuring out how the interactions mesh to create an application.

New Opportunities for Scaling and Resilience

Erlang and RESTful web services fit into a larger picture of recent technical changes that make it easier to apply Erlang's strengths.

Cloud Computing

Cloud computing, at least on the "Infrastructure as a Service" (IaaS) model, makes adding a new server to a network easy and fast. In a pre-cloud system, adding a new server would require ordering it, going to the data center, and physically installing it in a rack. Most cloud setups reduce that to a REST API that can start up a server in a minute or two.

This complements Erlang perfectly. Erlang has lots of features that allow a networked system to add nodes in real time and to detect when they fail. Of course, the specifics of how to set up an Erlang application in the cloud will depend a lot on the details of the application and what kind of loading it is expected to get.

 In IaaS cloud implementations the service provides virtual platforms, each of which runs a full OS. For use with Erlang that would probably be some form of Linux, but could also be Windows or some other OS.

Erlang provides a built-in function (BIF) called `erlang:monitor_node/2` that will send a message of the form `{nodedown, Node}` if the node in question goes offline. It would be simple to have the monitoring process use the REST API from AWS or another cloud provider to automatically bring up a new node in this case. It would also be possible to have the system bring up new nodes if the system is becoming overloaded.

There are two times when a system may wish to bring up one or more nodes. The first is when a node fails, and the system brings up a new node to replace it. The second is when a set of nodes is getting overloaded. This will of course take some system monitoring. But if a system is smart enough to know that the average system load over a set of nodes is increasing, then instead of crashing and letting the admin deal with it later, the system can be set up to create new nodes and link them into the system. The details of how to do this will vary depending on the hosting provider and the needs of the application.

It is probably also smart to include an option to override the automatic system and allow an admin to set a number of servers manually. For example, if your company is going to run an ad in the Super Bowl,[2] then it makes sense to have enough servers running and ready before the ad runs and the systems overload.

In addition to scaling out, there is also the issue of scaling down during those times when a system has more nodes than are needed. Your system may have been running up to 300 nodes to handle the load from the Super Bowl advertisement, but now that it's over it can be scaled back to a lower level. This is also useful for running the application on a test machine in development.

System Architecture and Erlang Scaling

From about 1970 to about 2002, system processors got faster, doubling in speed every 18 months or so. However, somewhere around 2002 something changed. As speeds kept getting faster, the laws of physics threw a brick in this progress. Faster speeds generate more heat, which uses more power and causes more problems in getting rid of waste heat. In addition, the speed of light puts a hard limit on how far a signal can travel in one clock cycle. Therefore, since 2002 the trend has not been to make processors faster but to put more of them on each chip.

When the CPUs were getting faster, it was pretty easy to speed up your code. If you just waited 18 months and did nothing, your program would go twice as fast! In the age of multi-core processors, this no longer works. Now programmers need to write programs that will use all the cores on a system. On a six-core chip, a sequential program can be running full steam on one core, but the other five are sitting around doing nothing.

As of the fall of 2011, Intel's high-end server chips have eight cores, the consumer chips from Intel have up to six cores (in many of those cases, each core can run two threads), and AMD has announced a line of processors with eight cores. IBM's Power7 chip has eight cores that run four threads each. It is not crazy to expect that in a few years we will be talking about chips with 32, 64, or even 128 cores or more. The way we write programs for these processors will be different from the way we wrote programs for the single-processor chips of the past. It is not clear that Erlang will scale to 64 or 128 cores, but it probably has a better chance to do so than most other languages.

If you want to use a multi-core chip efficiently, you need a large number of processes ready to run. Ideally the number of processes should be much larger than the number of chips to simplify distribution. If there are 16 processor threads running on the CPU, having only 16 or 32 processes will probably not work well, as statistically there needs to be a pool of processors waiting to run so that there is never a time when all the processes are blocked. There will be many times when the chip is doing nothing while

2. For those of you outside North America, the Super Bowl is the biggest festival of advertising in the United States each year. It also features a sporting event.

processes are waiting on the disk or network or the like. Having a large number of processes waiting means that the system can always have tasks in the queue when one process goes into a wait state.

Assuming that the time to switch between processes is very small (which for Erlang processes it is) then having several thousand processes or more would be best, so the system can make sure there are always processes to be thread into a waiting core.

The ability of a system like Erlang to scale well is dependent on three things: the speed at which processes are started, the speed at which the system can switch between them, and the cost for passing messages. Erlang does a good job minimizing all three of these factors.

Scaling up versus scaling out

There are two basic ways to scale a system: *up* or *out*. To scale a system up means to replace the server with a larger one—you take out the existing server and add in one with more CPUs, more memory, more disk, etc. There are limits to this, however, and it can be expensive. IBM's top-of-the-line servers can have as many as 32 CPUs with 1024 processor threads running at the same time. In web scale, however, that can still seem rather small.

To scale a system *out* means to spread it over a number of smaller servers. So instead of buying the million-dollar IBM Power7 server, you buy a bunch of Intel class servers and spread the work across them. The advantage of this is that if set up correctly, there are no limits besides the budget in how far it can scale. When used with today's cloud-based PaaS platforms, it can be possible to scale up for unexpected loads in minutes by ordering more servers from AWS or another cloud provider.

Amdahl's law

Gene Amdahl is a computer architect originally known for designing mainframes for IBM and others from the 1950s to the 1980s. He presented a strong argument about the nature of systems in which some parts are parallel and other parts are not.

This argument, known as Amdahl's law, states that in a system where parts of the process are sequential and other parts are parallel, then the total speedup can never be more than the parts that are sequential—adding more cores won't make the whole system go faster. (For a full explanation of Amdahl's law, see the Wikipedia page on the subject: *http://en.wikipedia.org/wiki/Amdahl%27s_law*.)

As an analogy, imagine that you go to a bank in which there are a bunch of tellers but only one cash counting machine. As more customers come in, the manager can always add more tellers, but if they must stand in line to use the cash counter the system will never get faster.

In any application, there will always be parts that are sequential. In an Erlang application, a few places come to mind. Module setup and tear down code is sequential, but as it will normally be run only when new services are being brought online, it is probably not a major source of bottlenecks.

One place that sequential resource uses can become a problem is access to disk. Disks are by definition sequential in that a given disk can be reading or writing only one thing at a time. The disk is also usually orders of magnitude slower than memory or CPU cache. Components like data stores that write data to disk or logging modules are often places where a bottleneck for the whole system can occur.

Another place that can cause a lot of sequential code is locks. In general, this is not an issue in Erlang the way it would be in Java or C#, but at least in theory it could be an issue with Mnesia or similar tools if things get blocked waiting for transactions.

Data Storage Options

Back in the "old days" of say, 1998 to 2005, the options for data storage when developing a web service was a choice of SQL databases. MySQL was always the easy choice; other options included Postgres, Oracle, and Microsoft SQL Server. All of these products are SQL databases, with all that is good and bad about SQL built into them.

SQL databases are very good for many things, but fail rather badly when it comes to horizontal scaling. Trying to build a partitioned database or a multi-master setup in most SQL databases is at best a major pain in the neck and at worst actively difficult. If Erlang and Yaws have been chosen for a project with the goal of having the service be fault tolerant and scalable, then of course those properties must be present in the data storage solution as well.

In the modern age, many web development projects are moving to "NoSQL," which is a loosely defined set of data storage technologies that have been created to deal with web-scale data. The good thing about NoSQL is that there are many more choices in terms of how data will be stored than there are in SQL. The bad thing is that since there are many more choices, the team developing an application must be ready to understand those choices and select the system or systems that will work best.

NoSQL solutions lack some SQL features that programmers have become used to. The first thing to note is that there is no idea of a join in most NoSQL data stores. Trying to join two tables across multiple hosts is a problematic task, requiring multiple phases of searching and joining using MapReduce techniques or something similar.

 For an overview of a number of SQL and NoSQL databases, check out the book *Seven Databases in Seven Weeks* by Eric Redmond and Jim R. Wilson (Pragmatic Programmers: *http://pragprog.com/book/rwdata/ seven-databases-in-seven-weeks*). This book discusses PostgreSQL, Riak, Redis, HBase, MongoDB, CouchDB, and Neo4j.

Many NoSQL data stores also lack any concept of a transaction. Ensuring consistency is up to the programmer. Again, this flows from the distributed nature of the data store. Trying to ensure that all the data across several hosts is always constant can often be an $O(N)$ or even $O(N^2)$ task. So it falls to the developer to ensure that data manipulations work in a sensible manner.

The other thing to be aware of when moving from SQL to NoSQL is that finding developers and system administrators who have been doing SQL for many years is relatively easy. There is a base of knowledge around SQL that has not yet been developed around NoSQL, which is still quite young. It is safe to say that 10 years from now SQL databases will look similar to the way they do today, while NoSQL still has a lot of evolution left simply because it is a new product family.

In order to be fault tolerant, a database, like an application server, must be able to scale to more than one computer and be able to handle the case where a server dies. In addition, to be scalable, each server must be independent. If with three nodes a cluster can serve N requests per minute, then with six nodes it should be able to serve 2N requests per minute (or at least close). In reality this is not usually possible, as contention for shared resources will get in the way. True linear scaling is a theoretical best case.

CAP Theorem

The CAP theorem is an idea proposed by Eric Brewer that states that it is impossible for a distributed computer system to provide strict guarantees on all three of Consistency, Availability, and Partition Tolerance *at the same time*. This theorem has in fact been mathematically proven to be true. A Google search will reveal the full details of the proof for those who may be interested.

A consistent system is one in which all nodes see the same data at all times. This is traditionally seen in single-node systems or those running on a small number of nodes. Most SQL databases feature extensive features in terms of transactions and the like to make sure that the data is always consistent at any given time, and in some cases this is an important feature.

It is possible to achieve consistency on massively concurrent systems; however, it must be done at the cost of fault tolerance or availability. In some cases the cost of achieving this may be quite high. In addition, if all nodes must agree on the state of data, this can making handling failures much harder as nodes can go offline.

The problem with a fully consistent system is that when scaling up to many nodes, the communication overhead can get very high. Every node must agree on all aspects of the state of the data at all times. This can make scaling systems difficult, as two-phase commits cause more and more locks to spread through the system.

However, full consistency is often not as important as people think. In many web scale applications, if some users see new data a few seconds after others, it does not matter that much—for example, if I post a new auction to eBay it's not terribly important if some users don't see it for a minute or two. On the other hand, in some banking systems this will matter a great deal.

An available system is one in which all clients can always read and write data. Obviously, having a system with guarantees about availability is a good thing; however, it is not possible to combine this with partition tolerance and constancy. If a system must be fully constant in the face of a network split, it must disallow writes as it will have no way to make sure the data is consistent across all nodes.

The best example of a partition-tolerant database is the DNS system. The DNS system is pretty much always available, but it is possible that some of the servers may be split from others at any given time, in which case they will serve up old data until the issue is resolved. Thus all users on the net will always be able to use the DNS system, but may not always see the same data for a given query.

The CAP theorem is mostly brought up in terms of databases, but in truth it applies to any distributed computing system. For example, Git and Mercurial version control tend to be AP systems, while CSV and Subversion tend to be CA systems. Systems like Git and Mercurial also need to explicitly handle the case where two sets of changes have to be merged.

In fact, the CAP theorem applies to many areas that might not be obvious. For example, foreign exchange is a widely available system that is not always exactly consistent. The price quotes in exchanges around the world will in general be similar, but may differ by a little bit and since it takes time for a signal to travel between London and New York, being 100% consistent would actually be impossible.

Erlang systems are by definition distributed, so CAP applies to not just the data store but the system as a whole. Understanding this idea is key to building a successful application in a distributed environment.

Mnesia

Mnesia is Erlang's own database. It is a very fast data store designed to work well with Erlang, and it has several nice advantages. It works with native Erlang records and code, and it is also possible to set it up to serve data from RAM or from disk and to mirror data across nodes. You can even set it up so that data lives in memory on most nodes but is mirrored to disk on one or two nodes, so that all access is in memory for very fast operations but everything is written out to disk for long-term persistence.

 Technically the Mnesia data store is ETS and DETS. Mnesia is a transaction and distribution layer built on top of them.

The one possible problem with Mnesia is that while it is not a SQL database, it is a CA database like a SQL database. It will not handle network partition. This does not mean that it is not usable in scalable applications, but it will have many of the same issues as SQL databases like MySQL.

Mnesia is built into Erlang so there is nothing to install. However, it must be started when Yaws is started. To do this, use the OTP function `application:start(mnesia).` to start up the Mnesia database. From here, tables can be created with the `mnesia:create_table/2` function, which uses Erlang records as its table schema. For full details of how to use Mnesia, see some of the Erlang references. The Erlang documentation also includes a set of man pages on Mnesia.

By using the `qlc` module, it is also possible to treat a Mnesia table as if it were a big array, so you can use Erlang's array comprehensions to pull data out of Mnesia. It is even possible to do things like `foldl` to summarize data in a table.

CouchDB

CouchDB is a data store that is actually written in Erlang. Unlike Mnesia and MySQL, CouchDB is not organized around records with a fixed schema; rather, it's a document store that takes some ideas from Lotus Notes. In fact, Damien Katz, who created CouchDB, used to work on Lotus Notes.

CouchDB also gives up strict consistency for an eventual consistency. By doing this, it can create guarantees of partition tolerance and availability. In a CouchDB network every node can be a master, and even if two nodes are not in communication, both can be updated.

This lack of consistency has some costs, but it also has some major benefits. In many cases, making sure all nodes agree about the state of data at all times is a very expensive operation that can create a lot of load on a large system.

There are multiple interfaces from Erlang to CouchDB, including couchbeam, eCouch, erlCouch, and erlang_couchdb. Each of these offers somewhat different features, but several of them (including couchbeam and eCouch) run as OTP applications. Links to all of these are available on the CouchDB wiki: *http://wiki.apache.org/couchdb/Getting _started_with_Erlang*.

MongoDB

MongoDB is also a NoSQL database, but it is designed to assume a consistent database with partition tolerance and the ability to share data easily. MongoDB can be accessed from Erlang with the emongo driver available from *https://bitbucket.org/rumataestor/ emongo*. The API is quite straightforward and documented at the website.

Redis

Redis is also a key value data store, but unlike MongoDB and CouchDB, Redis normally keeps its entire dataset in memory for very fast access, while keeping a journal of some form on disk so that it is still persistent across server restarts. Like Mongo, it is a CP data store.

There are two sets of drivers for Redis in Erlang, `Erldis` and `Eredis`, both of which can be found on the Redis home page at *http://redis.io*.

Riak

Riak is yet another document database that is similar to CouchDB in some ways. Like CouchDB, it is written in Erlang and gives up strict consistency for availability, scalability, and partition tolerance. It is meant to be a distributed system and has good support for scaling out by adding nodes~, and scaling back in by removing nodes that are no longer needed. Riak can be found at *http://www.basho.com*.

Riak is derived in large part from Amazon's Dynamo database. The idea is that you split many nodes over a consistent hashing ring, and any key in the database gets sent to the nodes taking charge of a given section of the ring.

The great thing about availability is that the nodes are split in a way that might allow a quorum system. That is to say that in a system of N nodes, for a write to be successful all the nodes must agree to the transaction. That is a fully consistent system with lower availability. If only some subset (M) of the nodes need to agree, then only a subset of the cluster has to be responsive for things to work.

By adjusting the ratio of M:N it is possible for a system to be tuned in terms of the level of consistency versus availability desired. This tuning can be set on a per-query basis so the system is very flexible.

As Riak is primarily written in Erlang, there is excellent support for interfacing Riak to Erlang applications.

CHAPTER 2

Getting Started with Yaws

Most developers who are moving from other web development environments to Erlang and Yaws will have used other web servers such as Nginx or Apache. The Erlang Yaws web server performs the same basic tasks, but the details of performing common actions are often different.

Erlang is not only a language, but also a runtime system and something that looks a lot like an application server. As such, Erlang and Yaws (or other web servers) will fill the same role as Apache/PHP/MySQL and other components all in one system.

The major differences between Erlang/Yaws and Apache/PHP have a lot to do with how Erlang tends to set things up. Erlang assumes that systems will be clustered, and processes in Erlang are somewhat different from those used in many other systems.

If you've used Apache with mod_php, you may remember that each request is handled by a process or thread (depending on how things are set up). The classic Common Gateway Interface (CGI) would start a new process for every request. These threads and processes are constructions of the OS and are relatively heavyweight objects. In Erlang the processes are owned not by the OS, but by the language runtime.

When building an application with Apache and PHP, for each request the web server must bring up a copy of the PHP interpreter and quite possibly recompile the various bits of PHP code that are to be run. This is an expensive operation. By comparison, in Yaws the Erlang code is probably already compiled and loaded, so in practice most of the time all Yaws will need to do is call the correct function.

An Erlang process is much more lightweight than an OS thread. The time it takes to start one, to send a message between them, or to context-switch them is much smaller than it would be with threads in C or Java, for example. This has some definite implications on how applications are designed. While Java will tend to use thread pools, in Erlang it is considered normal to just create a process for each client or socket because they are so inexpensive to use.

As Erlang processes are so lightweight and can be started up so quickly, Yaws can also create a new process for each request that comes in without any problem. This means that Yaws can scale up very well and quite quickly.

Working with Yaws

If you've never worked with Yaws, you have a few things to get used to. Yaws naturally sets up clusters, and it has its own way to create dynamic content and handle requests. Overall, however, Yaws is pretty easy to work with, and it uses the Erlang REPL so you can try code out at the command line.

Starting Yaws

Once Yaws is installed (see Appendix A) it must be started. To start Yaws at the Unix command line, simply run **yaws**. In Windows there are several options for starting Yaws from the Start menu, but the most common method is to open a DOS command window from the Start menu and do it from there.

There are a number of command-line switches that you can pass to Yaws. These let you set the node name or other options. This can also be done via the *.erlang* file, which Yaws will read when it first starts up. This file should contain valid Erlang code and should live in the user's home directory.

When Yaws is started it will print out a few lines of information that look similar to Example 2-1 and then drop into the Erlang REPL. At this point Yaws is fully functional and will serve any requests that you send it. It may take a second or two from when you start the Yaws executable to when it is ready to serve content to users.

By default, Yaws will be set up to listen on port 8000 (Example 2-1 changes it to 8081 due to something else using that port). Normally we want to run a web server on port 80 for HTTP or port 443 for HTTPS; however, many Unix-type systems will not allow nonroot users to bind to ports numbered below 1024. Clearly, running Erlang as root is probably not a good idea, so we need a different solution to this. It would be possible to run Yaws behind a catching proxy server that will map port 80 to a higher port. Alternatively, you could use a number of methods to attach to a higher port. Various ways of doing this are documented on the Yaws website at *http://yaws.hyber.org/priv bind.yaws*; you will need to figure out which one works best for your setup.

 The port that Yaws listens on is in a `<server>` block in the *yaws.conf* file. Each virtual host can listen on a different port or IP address, but they will all be able to access the same modules.

Example 2-1. YAWS at startup

```
Eshell V5.8.3  (abort with ^G)
(yaws@sag)1>
=INFO REPORT==== 1-Feb-2012::11:32:16 ===
Yaws: Using config file yaws.conf
(yaws@sag)1>
=ERROR REPORT==== 1-Feb-2012::11:32:16 ===
'auth_log' global variable is deprecated and ignored. it is now a per-server variable
(yaws@sag)1> yaws:Add path "/usr/lib/yaws/custom/ebin"
(yaws@sag)1> yaws:Add path "/usr/local/lib/yaws/examples/ebin"
(yaws@sag)1> yaws:Running with id="default" (localinstall=false)
Running with debug checks turned on (slower server)
Logging to directory "/var/log/yaws"
(yaws@sag)1>
=INFO REPORT==== 1-Feb-2012::11:32:17 ===
Ctlfile : /home/zkessin/.yaws/yaws/default/CTL
(yaws@sag)1>
=INFO REPORT==== 1-Feb-2012::11:32:17 ===
Yaws: Listening to 0.0.0.0:8081 for <1> virtual servers:
 - http://www:8081 under /home/zkessin/Writing/ErlangBook/yaws/DocRoot
(yaws@sag)1>
```

Unless you redirect them to a file, any logging commands sent by programs running in Yaws will appear in the Yaws startup code. You can also compile modules and test code here. In a system that needs to be kept running for a long period of time, it may be useful to start up the Yaws command line inside the Unix program screen, which will allow the session to be suspended and resumed later from a different computer. For testing and development I often run Yaws inside an Emacs shell buffer, from which I can easily copy and paste code from a scratch buffer to test things.

When you start up Yaws it reads a *yaws.conf* file. The default location of this file will vary depending on how Yaws was set up, but it can also be specified by a command-line switch. If you need to reload the *yaws.conf* file for some reason, you can do so by calling yaws --hup.

Serving Static Files

While web applications are built around dynamically generated content, almost all of them also have some static files that need to be served to clients. These will often be HTML, CSS, JavaScript, images, and other media. Yaws is capable of serving up static files, and as in Apache there is no special configuration needed: just place the files under the doc root and Yaws will happily push them out to the browser. (If Yaws is embedded inside a larger Erlang application, this may not be the case.)

A typical Yaws install will be spread over multiple nodes, so it is important that each node in a cluster have an up-to-date copy of each file. There are several ways to do this. If the cluster size is small (just a few nodes) then simply using rsync to copy files around may be a good solution. In a larger system, using the system's package manager along with a tool like Puppet (*http://puppetlabs.com*) to distribute the files may make sense.

It may also be possible to use a system like CouchDB to replicate resources around a network.

Using the CGI Interface

While it is best to use Yaws to manage code written in Erlang, you may find cases where using another language via the old-fashioned CGI interface still makes sense. Thankfully Yaws can do this quite well—simply configure the *yaws.conf* file to recognize files ending in *.cgi* or *.php* for correct handling.

In order to run scripts from Yaws, the `<server>` block in the *yaws.conf* file must have `allowed_scripts` set to include "php" or "cgi" as appropriate. The Yaws website has full details.

In addition, the `out/1` function can be set up to call a CGI function by invoking the `yaws_cgi:call_cgi/2` function, in the case where a CGI function should be called conditionally or otherwise need special handling.

Compiling, Loading, and Running Code

When you launch Yaws from a terminal, it will present a command-line REPL, which can be used to interact with Yaws and Erlang. This is a very easy way to play around with Yaws and try things out.

There are several ways to compile and load Erlang code. In testing, the easiest way is to type `c(module).` at the Yaws command line. This will compile the Erlang code down to a *.beam* file, which is Erlang's binary format, and load it into the Erlang system. Using `lc([module1, module2]).` will do the same with a list of modules. In general, the *.beam* files should be placed in directories in the code search path. In this case, when an unknown module is required, it will be loaded automatically. To explicitly load a *.beam* file compiled externally, `l(module).` will load the *.beam* file. (All of these take an atom, which is the name of the module. Other options from the shell may be found by running the `help/0` function from the Yaws command line.)

 Erlang programs run in a virtual machine, in the same way that Java and .NET programs do. In Erlang's case, the virtual machine was originally called "Bogdan's Erlang Abstract Machine" and is now "Bjorn's Erlang Abstract Machine" (Bogdan and Bjorn being the programmers who created them). As such, Erlang's binary object files have the extension *.beam*.

You can also change directories and view the current directory contents by using the `cd/1` and `ls/0` shell commands.

Example 2-2 shows a simple interaction in the Erlang shell. The shell is opened, we check the current directory with pwd/0, and then check the files in the directory with ls/0.

Example 2-2. ls and pwd

```
Erlang R14B02 (erts-5.8.3) [source] [64-bit] [smp:4:4] [rq:4] [async-threads:0] [kernel-
poll:false]

Eshell V5.8.3  (abort with ^G)
1> pwd().
/home/zkessin/Writing/ErlangBook/running
ok
2> ls().
.svn            example.erl     test.erl
ok
3> c(test).
{ok,test}
4> test:test(1234).
1234
5>
```

Then the test module, shown in Example 2-3, is compiled with the c/1 function. In this case the module compiled correctly, so it returns {ok,test}. If there were errors they would be reported here as well. Finally we run the test:test/1 function, which just returns its arguments.

Example 2-3. test.erl

```
-module(test).
-export([test/1]).
test(X) ->
    X.
```

The c/1 and l/1 functions will only load code on the current node. If you want to load code on all connected nodes, use the nc/1 and nl/1 functions. These work just like the single-node versions, but will propagate the changes out to all connected nodes.

The compile and load options mentioned above will also reload a module that is running. So it is easy to upgrade software; just reload it and make sure that functions are called with an explicit module name to do an upgrade (this can happen with an explicit message if desired).

In some cases—like if you're doing something larger involving make—compiling from the Yaws command line may not be the best choice. In that case there is an explicit Erlang compiler erlc,[1] which can be called from a Unix command line or from a build utility such as Make, Ant, or Maven. The modules can be explicitly loaded from a Yaws command-line switch or from the *yaws.conf* file. Normally an Erlang project is set up

---

1. The erlc executable and the command c/1 use the same code to do the actual compilation. Which one to use mostly depends on which is better for the programmer.

so that sources live in a *src* directory and the compiled files are moved to an *ebin* directory during the build process.

Erlang supports code autoloading. When a call is made to my_module:my_function/n, if the module my_module is not loaded then Erlang will attempt to load the module.

When Erlang attempts to load a module, it will look in its file path in a very similar way to how bash will find programs. You can see the contents of the Erlang path by running code:get_path() from the Erlang REPL. This will produce a result similar to Example 2-4. To add a new directory to the front of the path, call code:add_patha/1, and to add one to the end call code:add_pathz/1. Both will return true if the call is successful or {error, bad_directory} if not. Normally this should be done from an *.erlang* file in your home directory.

Example 2-4. Erlang path (Truncated)

```
(yaws@sag)16> code:get_path().
["/usr/local/lib/yaws/ebin",".",
 "/usr/lib/erlang/lib/kernel-2.14.3/ebin",
 "/usr/lib/erlang/lib/stdlib-1.17.3/ebin",
 "/usr/lib/erlang/lib/xmerl-1.2.8/ebin",
 "/usr/lib/erlang/lib/wx-0.98.9",
 "/usr/lib/erlang/lib/webtool-0.8.7/ebin",
 "/usr/lib/erlang/lib/typer-0.9/ebin",
 "/usr/lib/erlang/lib/tv-2.1.4.6/ebin",
 "/usr/lib/erlang/lib/tools-2.6.6.3/ebin",
```

Clustering Yaws

One of the major benefits of Erlang (and by extension, Yaws) is the fact that it is designed to exist in a clustered environment. The Yaws service itself can be clustered by simply starting it up on multiple nodes and then putting a standard load balancer in front of the web servers. However, in many cases the real power of Yaws will come from clustering a few nodes running Yaws with a larger Erlang application. As Yaws is native Erlang code, Yaws code can send and receive Erlang messages, which enables a Yaws application to exist inside an Erlang ecosphere.

In order for hosts to communicate, they must share a cookie value that should be kept secure. This cookie can be specified on the command line, set with an Erlang built-in function (BIF), or set in the *.erlang.cookie* file. Erlang will create that file with a random value if it is needed but not found. When setting up an Erlang network, finding a good way to distribute this cookie file is probably a good idea.

When working across multiple nodes one must be careful that the same code is always loaded on all nodes. Erlang has features to do that, such as the shell command lc/1, but will not load a new module on every node by default. While upgrading a system, the software must be able to deal with the case that some nodes may be running a newer or older version of the software.

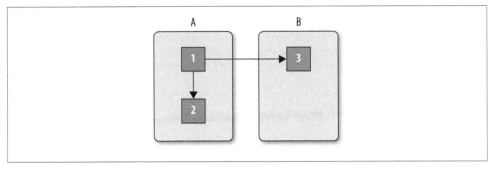

Figure 2-1. Cluster diagram

Setting up links between nodes in Erlang is actually quite easy. The first time a message is sent from one node to another, they will be connected together. So calling `net_admin:ping/1` or sending any other message will connect two nodes.

One nice thing about Erlang's processes is that when sending messages between them it does not matter where each process is running. The code `Pid ! message` sends `message` to the process `Pid`. `Pid` can be on the same computer, in a second Erlang process on the same host, on a different computer, or even on a computer running in a data center halfway around the world.

In Figure 2-1 there are two nodes—A and B; within those nodes, there are three processes numbered 1, 2, and 3. Messages can be sent between them via the ! operator (represented here with an arrow) regardless of where the two nodes are.

 In general, setting up cross–data center connections between nodes should use SSL tunneling, and may have a number of issues relating to delays between nodes.

Dynamic Content in Yaws

If the desired result is to output a page of HTML or XML, there are several good ways to go about this. If you give Yaws a file with the extension *.yaws*, it will look for any blocks in that file with the tag `<erl>` and run the `out/1` function that is found in that block. This is similar to how PHP will invoke code inside of a `<?php ?>` tag and how many other systems do templates. It is also possible to render HTML or XML with a template system like "ErlyDTL" (see "ErlyDTL" on page 26).

Yaws will in fact compile these files down to an *.erl* file, which will live in the `$HOME/.yaws` directory. If there is a syntax error the exact path will be given.

It is customary in Erlang to name a function with the name and parity. So out/1 is the function named "out" that takes one parameter, in this case a data structure that describes the request. The function out/2 would be a separate function that simply shares a name with out/1.

How Yaws Parses the File

When the browser requests a file with a *.yaws* extension, Yaws will read the file from the disk and parse that file. Any parts that are pure HTML will be sent to the browser.

However, anything in an **<erl>** block will be handled separately. Yaws will take each **<erl>** block and convert it into an Erlang module. Yaws will then compile the code and cache it in memory until the *.yaws* file is changed. As such, Yaws will not have to recompile the source except when the file is changed or first accessed.

Yaws will then call the function **out/1** and insert the return value of that function into the output stream. If there is an **<erl>** block without an **out/1** function, Yaws will flag it as an error.

If Yaws finds two or more **<erl>** blocks in a file, it will just convert each one into a module and compile and run them individually.

It is also important to note that unlike PHP, Yaws will not send any output to the socket until the entire page is processed. So it is possible to set a header from the bottom of the page after some HTML output has already been generated if that is needed.

If you want to understand the full process of how Yaws does all this, read the Yaws Internals Documentation at *http://yaws.hyber.org/internals.yaws* and the source code in *yaws_compile.erl*.

The **out/1** function is called with a parameter of an **#arg{}** record that is defined in the *yaws_api.hrl* file (see Example 2-5). All the data that might be needed to figure out details of the current HTTP request are here and can be used to determine what to do. This is the definition of the **#arg{}** record from the Yaws sources. In any *.yaws* files this will be automatically included; otherwise you will have to include it in the header of your module.

Example 2-5. Structure of the #arg{} record

```
-record(arg, {
        clisock,        %% the socket leading to the peer client
        client_ip_port, %% {ClientIp, ClientPort} tuple
        headers,        %% headers
        req,            %% request
        clidata,        %% The client data (as a binary in POST requests)
        server_path,    %% The normalized server path
                        %% (pre-querystring part of URI)
        querydata,      %% For URIs of the form ...?querydata
                        %%  equiv of cgi QUERY_STRING
        appmoddata,     %% (deprecated - use pathinfo instead) the remainder
```

```
                      %% of the path leading up to the query
    docroot,          %% Physical base location of data for this request
    docroot_mount,    %% virtual directory e.g /myapp/ that the docroot
                      %%  refers to.
    fullpath,         %% full deep path to yaws file
    cont,             %% Continuation for chunked multipart uploads
    state,            %% State for use by users of the out/1 callback
    pid,              %% pid of the yaws worker process
    opaque,           %% useful to pass static data
    appmod_prepath,   %% (deprecated - use prepath instead) path in front
                      %%of: <appmod><appmoddata>
    prepath,          %% Path prior to 'dynamic' segment of URI.
                      %%  ie http://some.host/<prepath>/<script-point>/d/e
                      %% where <script-point> is an appmod mount point,
                      %% or .yaws,.php,.cgi,.fcgi etc script file.
    pathinfo          %% Set to '/d/e' when calling c.yaws for the request
                      %% http://some.host/a/b/c.yaws/d/e
                      %%  equiv of cgi PATH_INFO
}).
```

In Example 2-6, the HTTP method is extracted from the #arg{} structure and then returned to be rendered into HTML, as shown in Figure 2-2.

Example 2-6. Using ARG

```
<erl>
method(Arg) ->
  Rec = Arg#arg.req,
  Rec#http_request.method.

out(Arg) ->
  {ehtml, f("Method: ~s" , [method(Arg)])}.
</erl>
```

Figure 2-2. Output of Example 2-6

It is also possible to define your actual logic in a set of modules that are compiled and loaded normally into Erlang and then use a set of *.yaws* files to invoke those functions from the Web. To do this, use a *.yaws* file like that shown in Example 2-7. This has an out/1 function that simply calls my_module:some_func/1, which does the actual work. This way the actual logic can be held in normal Erlang modules but without the complexity of appmods (see Chapter 3). Just remember to export the needed functions from the Erlang modules.

Example 2-7. Calling an external function

```
<erl>
out(Arg) ->
    my_module:some_func(Arg).
</erl>
```

In Example 2-8, we use the yaws_api:parse_post/1 function to return a list of the options sent over HTTP via POST. There is also a function yaws_api:parse_query/1 that will return data sent in the query string as in an HTTP GET operation.

Example 2-8. Displaying POST variables

```
<erl>
out(Arg) ->
  {ehtml, f("~p", [yaws_api:parse_post(Arg)])}.
</erl>
```

There are a number of options for what out/1 can return. If it returns a tuple like {html, "Hello World"}, the string will be inserted literally into the HTML document.

EHTML

Among the options for return types from out/1 is {ehtml, DATA}, where "ehtml" is a Domain Specific Language (DSL) that allows you to map Erlang data structures onto HTML elements. Each element of an EHTML data structure should look like {Tag, Attributes, Content}, and of course the content can be further EHTML records so the entire EHTML structure is recursive.

Example 2-9. EHTML example

```
{table, [],
 {tr, [{class, "row"}],
  [{td, [], "Hello World"}]}}
```

The EHTML shown in Example 2-9 will produce the HTML shown in Example 2-10. EHTML can also be used to produce XML if needed for web services.

Example 2-10. EHTML example output

```
<table>
<tr class="row">
<td>Hello World</td></tr></table>
```

In all *.yaws* pages, Yaws includes the function `f/2`, which is an alias for the function `io_lib:format/2`. This function is similar to the C function `sprintf()` except that it uses "~" instead of "%" for formatting, which is to say that it takes a formatted string and a list of arguments and returns a formatted string. For full details of all the options, see the Erlang manual page at *http://www.erlang.org/doc/man/io_lib.html#format-2*.

Headers and Redirects

There are times when a web application will wish to set one or more custom headers to send back with the content of the request. To do this, return the tuple {`header`, `HeaderString`}. For example, {`header`, `"X-Server: Yaws"`} will send back "X-Server: Yaws" as a header.

To return HTML as well as multiple headers, just put the tuples in a list in the return values. Example 2-11 will cause Yaws to return a response similar to Example 2-12.

Example 2-11. Headers and content

```
<erl>
out(Arg) ->
    [{html, "Header with HTML"},
     {header, "X-Server: Yaws"}].
</erl>
```

Example 2-12. Headers and content response

```
HTTP/1.1 200 OK
Server: Yaws 1.90
Date: Fri, 30 Dec 2011 08:50:32 GMT
Content-Type: text/html
X-Server: Yaws

Header with HTML
```

There are a few headers that are so common that Yaws provides a shorthand method of sending them. You can set the headers `connection`, `location`, `cache_control`, `set_cookie`, `content_type`, or `content_length` with the following format: {`content_length`, `4312`}; that is, as a simple pair of atom and value.

In addition, by returning the tuple {`status`, `Code`}, Yaws allows you to send back a status other than "200 OK". So it is possible to send back "201" for a resource created or "405" if the user sent a request with an illegal method. To do this, return {`status`, `201`}.

To redirect the user to a different URI from the `out/1` function, return the tuple {`redirect`, `URL`}. Yaws will send back a HTTP 302 Found response, which will cause the browser to redirect to the new URI. See Example 2-13.

Example 2-13. Redirect

```
<erl>
out(Arg) ->
    URL = "http://www.erlang.org",
    {redirect, URL}.
</erl>
```

The HTTP standards require a full URL for requests (see Example 2-13). However, in many cases the redirect may be from one resource on a server to another on the same server, so using a relative URI may make sense. Fortunately Yaws provides a way to do this by returning {redirect_local, RELATIVE_URI}, as in Example 2-14. Of course, in both of these cases, the choice of whether to redirect as well as the location to redirect to do not have to be fixed at compile time.

Example 2-14. Local redirect

```
<erl>
out(Arg) ->
    RELATIVE_URI = "/some_other_file.yaws",
    {redirect_local, RELATIVE_URI}.
</erl>
```

 If in development you get stuck in redirect confusion, try using curl to sort things out. It will allow you to see each redirect that the server sends back and figure out what went wrong. To make curl redirect, pass it the --location option.

Templates

In addition to EHTML and the f/2 function described in "Dynamic Content in Yaws" on page 21, there are several template packages available on Erlang. These template engines allow the developer to separate HTML from data processing, which is always good practice. This is nice because it frees you from needing to have the structure of the returned Erlang data match the exact structure that will be shown on screen to a user. It also provides a powerful and well known set of transformations to convert the output of the Erlang functions to the HTML that the user can see.

ErlyDTL

If you are familiar with the Python Django template library, you'll want to check out the ErlyDTL package. ErlyDTL is a port of the Django template library to Erlang, and you can find it on GitHub at *https://github.com/evanmiller/ErlyDTL*. Full documentation for ErlyDTL can be found there, and the full documentation for the Django template library can be found at the Django website: *https://www.djangoproject.com/*.

The ErlyDTL `compile/2` function takes a template—which can be a string that will be interpreted as a path to a file or a literal template as a binary and a module name—and convert it into a compiled Erlang module with a few defined function that can be used to render the template and get some information about it. There is also a `compile/3` function that allows the developer to specify options for the compilation.

To compile a template as in Example 2-15, first load the ErlyDTL package (line 2). In this case it was necessary to first change Erlang's search path with `code:add_patha/1`. After that, in line 4, `ErlyDTL:compile/2` compiles the templates.

Example 2-15. Compiling ErlyDTL templates

```
(yaws@sag)1> code:add_patha("<root>/templates/erlydtl/ebin").
true
(yaws@sag)2> l(erlydtl).
{module,erlydtl}
(yaws@sag)3> cd("templates").
/home/zkessin/Writing/ErlangBook/yaws
ok
(yaws@sag)4> erlydtl:compile("<root>/templates/hello-world.dtl", hello_world).
ok
```

Building ErlyDTL as Part of a Make Process

In Example 2-15, the template is compiled on the Erlang REPL, which is great for testing things out and making sure that they work correctly. However, a real project will probably need to do something like continuous integration and will require a different solution to building ErlyDTL templates.

In this case, templates should be located in their own directory and compiled with the script in Example 2-16 as part of the build process. The script will compile the templates down to *.beam* files that can be loaded as any other module.

This script should be called like in Example 2-15 and can be called from Make, Emake, or your build system of choice. As long as the *.beam* is in Erlang's search path it will be loaded when needed.

```
erlydtl_compile templates/hello_world.dtl hello_world ebin
```

Example 2-16. ErlyDTL compile script

```
#!/usr/bin/env escript
-export([main/1]).

main([File_Name, Module, BinDir]) ->
    l(erlydtl),
    erlydtl:compile(File_Name,
            Module,
            [{out_dir,BinDir}]).
```

This script uses `escript`, which is a method of doing shell scripts in Erlang. The full details are beyond the scope of this book, but the condensed version is that when run, the `main/1` function is called with a list of parameters passed on the command line.

The ErlyDTL template, when compiled, will appear to Erlang as a module that exports a few functions. The most basic form is `template:render/1`, which will return `{ok, Content}` or `{error, Error}`. There is also a `template:render/2` version that allows some customization of the template function. It is possible to pass a locale, a translation function that will work on `{% trans %}` tags. For a full list of options, see the ErlyDTL web page.

ErlyDTL will take a Django template and compile it down to an Erlang *.beam* file with standard functions for the templates that can be used just like any other functions.

Django templates put symbols in double bracket escaping, as in Example 2-17.

Example 2-17. A simple DTL template

```
<h1>Hello {{ planet }}</h1>
```

After the template has been compiled, it can be called with the `module:render/1` function as in Example 2-18.

Example 2-18. Calling the template

```
<erl>
out(Arg) ->
    {ok,HTML} = hello_world:render([{planet, "Earth"}]),
    {html, HTML}.
</erl>
```

Note that the `render/1` function returns `{ok, HTML}` while `out/1` should return something like `{html, HTML}`, so it is necessary to unwrap the results of the render function and rewrap them with a different atom. The server will return output like in Example 2-19 to the browser.

Example 2-19. Template output

```
<h1>Hello Earth </h1>
```

When invoking a Django template, the data to be passed in is sent as a list of pairs of the form `{Key, Value}` where the `Key` is normally an Erlang atom. So in Example 2-18 the passed value is `[{planet, "Earth"}]`. If there are multiple values, you can pass them in as a list. In addition, the value does not need to be a simple string, but could be a data structure of some form that will be processed by the template to produce a list or some other content.

Not Quite Working Right

When something goes wrong in a Yaws request, it will show a screen like Figure 2-3. In this case, the template has malfunctioned.

`hello_world:render/1` was not found because the module had not been loaded.

When ErlyDTL compiles a *.dtl* file, it will by default load the code into the Erlang Virtual Machine but will not save a *.beam* file so that you have to specify the option `out_dir` as part of the compile, which will tell ErlyDTL where to store the *.beam* files. If not specified, it will not create them.

Figure 2-3. Django template not quite working

Django templates can of course do more than just interpolate variables as in Example 2-17. It is also possible to include display logic in your templates. For example, you can have logic to iterate over a list by using `{% for i in somelist %}` and within that to have alternate rows be styles by using logic like `{% cycle odd even %}`.[2]

You can also use ErlyDTL to build XML as well as HTML files, as shown in Example 2-20.[3] Here the template iterates over a list of articles and pulls data out of each field in the `#article` record to build an XML document for an RSS feed.

---

2. It is also possible to have alternate styles on rows by using CSS selectors like `:nth-child(even)` and `:nth-child(odd)`, so there are multiple ways to do that. However, `cycle` can be used in other places and so should not be discounted.

3. This is taken from Fred Hebert's "blogerl" project. Fred was nice enough to allow me to use this example here.

Example 2-20. RSS template

```
<?xml version="1.0"?>
<rss version="2.0">
  <channel>
    <title>Ferd.ca</title>
    <link>{{ url.base }}</link>
    <description>My own blog about programming and whatnot.</description>
    <language>en-us</language>
    <pubDate>{{ latest_date }}</pubDate>
    <lastBuildDate>{{ latest_date }}</lastBuildDate>
    <ttl>60</ttl>

    {% for article in articles %}
    <item>
      <title>{{ article.title }}</title>
      <link>{{ url.base }}{{ article.slug }}.html</link>
      <description>{{ article.desc }}</description>
      <pubDate>{{ article.date }}</pubDate>
      <guid>{{ url.base }}{{ article.slug }}.html</guid>
    </item>
    {% endfor %}

  </channel>
</rss>
```

A full tutorial on the Django template library is beyond the scope of this book, but it can be found at *https://docs.djangoproject.com/en/dev/ref/templates/builtins/*. This documents all of the various forms that can be used in DTL.

 There are other Erlang template engines floating around the Web besides ErlyDTL. Each has its own strong and weak points, so you'll want to look around for the best solution to a specific problem.

Logging

Of course any web server needs to be able to log data, which can be used to analyze errors as well as for reasons like business intelligence.

Yaws will create a number of log files by default. Where these files live can be configured in the *yaws.conf* file, but normally they will be somewhere like */var/log/yaws*.

The first log is the access log, which is presented in the same format that Apache and a number of other web servers save their log files. See Example 2-21. (Note that this would normally be all on one line but has been wrapped over several to fit the page in this book.)

Example 2-21. Access log

```
127.0.0.1 - - [24/Feb/2012:11:31:02 +0200] "GET /templates/hello-world.yaws HTTP/1.1" 500
774
"-" "Mozilla/5.0 (X11; Linux x86_64) AppleWebKit/535.7 (KHTML, like Gecko)
Ubuntu/11.10 Chromium/16.0.912.77 Chrome/16.0.912.77 Safari/535.7"
```

Also, any errors that are reported in Yaws will be reported in the file */var/log/yaws/report.log* in a format that looks somewhat like Example 2-22.

Example 2-22. Report log

```
=INFO REPORT==== 20-Sep-2011::13:49:39 ===
Yaws: Listening to 0.0.0.0:8080 for <1> virtual servers:
 - http://localhost:8080 under /usr/share/yaws

=ERROR REPORT==== 24-Sep-2011::19:15:26 ===
Yaws: bad conf: Expect directory at line 130 (docroot: /var/www/yaws) terminating
```

As we have seen in prior examples, if you call `io:format/1` it will send the string to the Yaws console. This is useful for testing and such but is not captured for later use. What is really needed is a package that will log messages to a file on disk or other central point for later collection and analysis.

Erlang OTP error_logger

Erlang provides a standard `error_logger` package as part of OTP that allows the programmer to send the normal `info`, `warning`, and `error` levels.

 Erlang processes direct their console IO to the console of their group leader. By default, this will be the process that started up that process (or recursively up to a console); however, it is possible to change this. See the Erlang manual for more information.

The error logger is a standard part of the Erlang/OTP kernel and will always be present. By default it will send errors to the tty; however, by setting the `error_logger` parameter to `{file, FileName}` it will send errors to the named file. It is also possible to set the value of `error_logger` to `silent` to turn off error reporting altogether.

To send an error message call `error_logger:error_msg/1` or `error_logger:error_msg/2`. The first version takes a literal string that is sent to the error message as is. The second version takes a string and a list of parameters that will be interpolated into that string. The formats for this are the same as in `io:format/2`, which resembles C's "sprintf" but with the percent signs replaced by tildes.

Demonstrating the use of logs in an Erlang program, Example 2-23 shows a basic info log statement in a *.yaws* file.

Example 2-23. Code with logging

```
<erl>
out(Arg) ->
    error_logger:info_msg("~p:~p User Entered the System~n",
                [?MODULE,?LINE]),
    {html, "Logger"}.
</erl>
```

It will produce output like in Example 2-24 on the console or in a file, depending on how the system is set up.

Example 2-24. Log message

```
=INFO REPORT==== 16-Jan-2012::13:38:52 ===
m1:13 User Entered the System
```

The macros ?MODULE and ?LINE expand to the current module and the current line in that file. So by putting them in the log statement it is possible to see where the log message was generated. As it was from a *.yaws* file in this example, the module will resolve to something like m1 and the line will not be the actual line of the *.yaws* file.

The functions error_logger:warning_msg/1,2 and error_logger:info_msg/1,2 work exactly the same as the error_msg/1,2 functions, but for a different level of errors.

CHAPTER 3

Appmods: Dynamic Content in Yaws

When developing a web service, there are times when the developer does not want to map the URL that is sent by the web browser to an actual file. This may be because all data is stored in a database or is generated dynamically. In this case you want the browser to go to some URL and have the server create the content and return it.

Appmods are to Yaws what Apache modules are to Apache—a way to create a custom handler for a URL in the web server. When using an appmod, the browser will send a standard URL, but instead of having a static file sent back to the user, Yaws will execute some Erlang code and send the response back to the user. This allows for fully dynamic content in the Yaws web server.

The difference is that in the case of an appmod, `out/1` will need to create the full content of the response, while in a *.yaws* file it may just be a small part of it. In many cases, the response will not be HTML but will be some other format, such as XML ("XML" on page 49), JSON ("JSON" on page 47), or even something like an audio file, CSV text file, or PDF.

In addition, by using an appmod you can break the association between a file on the local disk of a node and the URL representation that is presented. So it is possible to present a URL like `/blog-posts/2011-Dec-02/why-you-should-use-erlang.html` without there actually being a file at that path (or even a directory structure)—just some code that knows how to map that URL onto some logical resource that can then be constructed. Similar effects can be achieved with mod_rewrite in Apache or with other Apache modules.

In the case of a binary format, then, Erlang should create the data and return it with the correct header. The specifics of how to create a binary will depend on the format of the data and are beyond the scope of this book. However, in many cases there will be Erlang modules to create the data; in some cases the data will be streamed to the client.

If an appmod is set up at the root of the web server, then with a request to `http://example-server.com/chatroom/example-room.json` the `Arg#arg.appmoddata` field will be set to /chatroom/example-room.js, which is the part of the path to be handled by the appmod.

It is also possible to set up the appmod to handle only a subset of the web server, in which case the path passed to the appmod will be just the end of the URI and will be in Arg#arg.appmod_prepath.

Appmod Configuration

To set up an appmod, add an appmods field to the <server> block in yaws.conf. The general format of this is shown in Example 3-1.

The basic form of the appmods configuration is <path, module>. The path can be any path on the web server. If you want the appmod, serve all content from the web server, set the path to "/", which will route all requests to the appmod. However, even in this case you'll probably want some directories to be served as static files, (for example, the images directory), so it is possible to add a list of paths to be excluded with the exclude_paths directive, as in Example 3-1.

Example 3-1. Appmod config options

```
appmods = <path, module exclude_paths icons css js>
```

In this case, any path called that was not in the *icons*, *css*, or *js* directories will be routed to the function module:out/1. Here the out/1 function works the same as in "Dynamic Content in Yaws" on page 21.

When the URI Does Not Correspond to a File

In the case of *.yaws* files, the HTTP path sent to the server will map directly onto the file. The user will make a request like "/get-stock-price.yaws" and Yaws will invoke the code in the file *get-stock-price.yaws*.

However, in an appmod the programmer has to translate the request URI into some action directly. This transfers some workload from the web server to the developer, but it is not overly hard to do.

In order to do this we need to find out what URI the user requested from within our handler function. This can be set in one of several places in the #arg record. It will be in pathinfo or in fullpath (actually both).

In general, the path info will be a set of strings separated by slashes, so a request to /record.yaws/show/3141/5926 will have pathinfo set to show/3141/5926. This string should be split with re:split/3 and then used to show the correct data.

This path can be split up into individual tokens by using re:split/2 or string:tokens/2. As shown in Example 3-2, both of these will take the string and a token or regular expression to split up the string and return a list. However, there is a slight difference.

The `re:split/2` function will return a list of binaries and will leave the empty string at the start of the list. On the other hand, `string:tokens/2` will return a list of strings and will not include the initial blank element.

Example 3-2. Splitting a string

```
1> T = "/show/3141/5926".
"/show/3141/5926"
2> re:split(T, "/").
[<<>>,<<"show">>,<<"3141">>,<<"5926">>]
3> string:tokens(T, "/").
["show","3141","5926"]
```

In Example 3-3, the `path/1` function splits the `appmoddata` path from the arg record on the directory separator character ("/") and then uses a case statement to match the path against various options that will provide correct handlers depending on details of what is passed. The patterns can match specific strings or have array elements assigned to variables. Patterns will match from top to bottom until one matches or no pattern matches, which will case the process to crash. A full description of pattern matching is beyond the scope of this book, but the concept is very important for programming in Erlang.

By adding the term `[{return,list}, trim]` to the `re:split/3` function, it will drop any empty elements, and return the result as a list of strings and not in a binary format.

Example 3-3. Path

```
path(Path) ->
    Elements = re:split(Path,"/", [{return, list}, trim]),
    case Elements of
        ["ChatRooms", Room] ->
            act_on_room(Room);
        [Directory, File] ->
            show_file(Directory, File);
        [Directory] ->
            show_directory(Directory)
    end.
```

Cookies

When the World Wide Web was first created back in the 1990s, each HTTP request was independent and web requests had no ability to maintain any form of state. So for example, a web server had no easy way to keep track of items in a user's shopping cart.

Netscape introduced cookies in an early version of Navigator and they are now standard in all modern browsers. A cookie can be set by the browser or the server, and once set will be sent in the headers of all HTTP requests to that server until it expires or is removed. Yaws can of course set cookies and access them.

In general, cookies are used to track the activities of a user on a website. This can include authentication as well as state. For example, if the site implements a shopping cart, the user's current items can be tracked by a cookie. It is usually best to not put the items themselves in the cookie, but to put a hash that can refer to a database record that contains the cart information. This will greatly reduce the bandwidth used by the application.

HTTP cookies are a form of persistent data that can be set by the browser or the server and will accompany every request sent to the server. To set a cookie, use `yaws_api:set cookie/2`, which takes the cookie name and value. If you want to set options for the cookie, check out the yaws_api man page, that has versions of `yaws_api:setcookie/n` which take extra parameters to allow you to specify a bunch of other options.

 Do not confuse the HTTP cookies discussed here with the cookies that Erlang uses to provide security when connecting nodes.

You can also set a cookie by having `out/1` return `{set_cookie, Cookie}`, since cookies are part of the HTTP headers.

To get the existing cookies, look at the `headers` record of the `Arg` record. The function `yaws_api:find_cookie_val/2` can extract the value of a cookie from the list of cookies, as in Example 3-4. If a cookie is not set, this function will return empty HTML.

Example 3-4. Cookies

```
<erl>
out(Arg) ->
    Headers = Arg#arg.headers,
    Cookie  = Headers#headers.cookie,
    Prefs =  yaws_api:find_cookie_val("Prefs", Cookie),
    {html, Prefs}.
</erl>
```

Yaws also includes a set of interfaces to create session tracking with cookies (see "Session Handling" on page 36).

Session Handling

Yaws provides a nice API for handling sessions with cookies with the `yaws_api:new_cookie_session/1-3` functions. The basic function `new_cookie_session/ 1` takes a state record that can be specified by the application. This record can be retrieved by the function `yaws_api:cookieval_to_opaque/1`.

To update the session data, use the function `yaws_api:replace_cookie_session/2` with the name of the cookie and the new state value.

In addition to the new_cookie_session/1 function, there is also a new_cookie_session/2 that takes a timeout (TTL) value after which the cookie session will be cleared. In new_cookie_session/1 the session will time out after a default period of time.

If some form of cleanup after a session ends is desired, use the new_cookie_session/3 function. In addition to a state variable and a TTL, this function also takes a PID for a cleanup process. When a session ends, it will send that process a message of the form {yaws_session_end, Reason, Cookie, Opaque}. Reason can be timeout or normal.

To remove a session, use the delete_cookie_session/1 function, which will remove the cookie and send a cleanup message if needed.

In Example 3-5, which is taken from the Yaws sources, there is an example of session handling. Similar to the way PHP treats the $_SESSION construct, Yaws does not actually save the record to the HTTP cookie but will instead store a key of the form nonode@nohost-5560960749617266689 and store the cookie on the server. Normally the cookie and data will be stored in the Yaws processes; however, you can set it to store in a Mnesia or ETS data store. There are examples for this at *http://yaws.hyber.org/pcookie.yaws*.

Example 3-5. Cookie session handling (session.erl)

```
-record(myopaque, {udata,
                   times = 0,
                   foobar}).

out(A) ->
    H = A#arg.headers,
    C = H#headers.cookie,
    case yaws_api:find_cookie_val("baz", C) of
        [] ->
            M = #myopaque{},
            Cookie = yaws_api:new_cookie_session(M),
            Data = {ehtml,
                    {html,[],
                     ["I just set your cookie to ", Cookie, "Click ",
                      {a, [{href,"session1.yaws"}], " here "},
                      "to revisit"]}},
            CO = yaws_api:setcookie("baz",Cookie,"/"),
            [Data, CO];
        Cookie ->
            case yaws_api:cookieval_to_opaque(Cookie) of
                {ok, OP} ->
                    OP2 = OP#myopaque{times = OP#myopaque.times + 1},
                    yaws_api:replace_cookie_session(Cookie, OP2),
                    Data = {ehtml,
                            {html,[],
                             [
                              "Click ",
                              {a, [{href,"session1.yaws"}], " here "},
                              "to revisit",
                              {p, [], f("You have been here ~p times",
                                        [OP2#myopaque.times])},
```

```
                                {p, [], f("Your cookie is ~s", [Cookie])}]}},
                    Data;
                {error, no_session} ->
                    new_session()
            end
    end.


new_session() ->
    M = #myopaque{},
    Cookie = yaws_api:new_cookie_session(M),

    Data = {ehtml,
            {html,[],
            ["I just set your cookie to ", Cookie, "Click ",
            {a, [{href,"session1.yaws"}], " here "},

            "to revisit"]}},
    CO = yaws_api:setcookie("baz",Cookie,"/"),
    [Data, CO].
```

Access Control

Sometimes you may wish to to restrict access to resources, for example to users who have entered a password or can otherwise be authenticated (as in a Facebook application). In many cases you may wish to do something like check a username and password or session token against a Mnesia database or other data store.

Ideally you would validate the username and password against some source of data, such as a Mnesia table. In Example 3-6, I use the function validate_username_password/ 1 that extracts the username and password from the request and checks them against the Mnesia table. This function will return either {true, Uuid} if the user authenticates correctly, or {false, Reason}. In this case, Reason can be no_user in the case where there is no user by that name, or bad_password. Clearly sharing the reason why the login was rejected would be a bad idea.

The out/2 function takes the result of validate_username_password/1 and returns either {status, 401} if the user did not authenticate or a HTML page. It also logs the login attempt.

Example 3-6. Custom access control (access-control.erl)

```
-module('access-control').
-include("../roulette/yaws_api.hrl").
-export([out/1]).
-record(user,
    {
      uuid,
      username,
      passwordMD5
    }).
```

```
validate_username_password(Arg) ->
    Username = yaws_api:queryvar(Arg, "Username"),
    Password = yaws_api:queryvar(Arg, "Password"),
    PasswordMD5 = crypto:md5(Password),
    Query = fun () ->
            mnesia:read({username, Username})
        end,
    Value = mnesia:transaction(Query),
    case Value of
    {atomic, []} ->
        {false, no_user};
    {atomic, [UserRecord]}
      when UserRecord#user.passwordMD5 =:= PasswordMD5 ->
        {true, UserRecord#user.uuid};
     {atomic, [_UserRecord]} ->
        {false, bad_password}
    end.

out({false, Reason}, _Arg) ->
    io:format("~p:~p Unable to login user: ~p", [?MODULE, ?LINE, Reason]),
    {status, 401};
out({true, Uuid}, _Arg) ->
    io:format("~p:~p Welcome: ~p", [?MODULE, ?LINE, Uuid]),
    {html, "Hello World"}.

out(Arg) ->
    out(validate_username_password(Arg), Arg).
```

Interacting with Erlang Services and Business Logic Layers

In many cases a web service will be a simple wrapper around a more complex middle layer made up of OTP servers, which can be communicated with by Erlang's standard message passing methods.

To do this, Yaws must be clustered with the other Erlang nodes and must know the PID of the process to communicate with. Example 3-7 shows how to make this work.

Example 3-7. Interacting with middleware

```
out(Arg) ->
    BackendPid ! {webrequest, node(), Arg}
    receive
        {response, Data} ->
            Data;
        {error, ErrorMsg} ->
            ErrorMsg
    after 500 ->
        [
        {status, 404},
        {html, "<h2>System timed out</h2>"}]
    end.
```

There are a few things here to note. First of all, sending messages never fails, but there is no guarantee of delivery. So if the process has gone away for some reason, the send will not return any sort of error. Therefore the code in Example 3-7 must have a timeout to let the user know that something went wrong. In this case it is the after clause, which will wait 500ms and then return a timeout error.

A better way to handle this would be to wrap the middleware in a gen_server and use the OTP framework to create a number of custom servers to run the application. This is done in Chapter 9. In this case, each module will export a set of access functions that can be called and will use the OTP gen_server:call/2 or gen_server:cast/2 functions to access the server infrastructure. The implementation of gen_server takes care of all of the message passing so the ! operator is never explicitly used.

Compare Example 3-7 to Example 3-8. In the former, all the nonfunctional parts have been hidden by gen_server:call/2, which is well-tested and can be assumed to work correctly. In the latter, our out/1 function does not need to know anything about the operation of the layer it is calling; it just calls the get_data/1 function, which serves as an interface to some form of backend service.

Example 3-8. Interacting with a service via OTP

```
get_data(Req) ->
    {response, Data} = gen_server:call(?MODULE, Req),
    Data.
```

CHAPTER 4

Implementing REST

So far this book has focused on the parts of how to build a web service, such as how to use a template and respond to a request. It is now time to expand our view to building larger, more complex integrated services to deal with complex business requirements.

In this chapter I will show how to build a simple RESTful service to store a list of airports. The service will use GET to request a list of airports, POST to add a new airport, PUT to update an airport, and DELETE to remove one.

This chapter will focus on the technical aspects of how to take an HTTP request in to some Erlang code and turn it into the correct output data or server actions. So, for example, the user may send an HTTP POST to create a new airport record, and the code will then store that data in a Mnesia database.

 Most of what is in this chapter also applies to any form of web services insofar as they require the server to examine the incoming request and make an appropriate response.

Decoding a Request

When an HTTP request is made to the server there are a number of pieces of data that come with that request. All of these are sent to the out/1 function via the Arg data structure, and they can be extracted from that data structure. In some cases there are preexisting functions to extract the data, in others you will have to create functions to extract what you need.

Extracting the User's Request

It is important to understand how a web browser or other client sends data to the server. In the case of a GET or HEAD request, data is sent via the URL and query string, so a request could look something like get-stock-price?stock=ibm. There are two pieces of information here: the first is the path of the command get-stock-price, and the second is the query string stock=ibm. For those of you who are familiar with PHP this would be delivered by the $_GET variable. In a POST or PUT request, in addition to the query string, data can also be sent in the body of the request.

 We could also make this request as /get-stock-price/ibm, which has the advantage of the fact that there is no query string (the bit after the "?"), and most implementations of the HTTP standard, including proxy servers and browser, do not cache GET requests that have a query string. We saw how to deal with this type of request in "When the URI Does Not Correspond to a File" on page 34.

For values sent via GET or POST there are simple functions to extract data. The functions parse_query/1 and parse_post/1 take the Arg data record and return a list of tuples of the form [{Key, Value}]. So if the request URL ends with ...?record=31415926, then parse_query/1 will return {"record", "31415926"}.

If instead of getting the entire list of parameters the code only cares about a specific value, use the yaws_api:postvar/2 or yaws_api:queryvar/2 functions. These functions will be imported automatically in all ".yaws" pages, and so can be used without the yaws_api: prefix. These functions will return {ok, Value} if the variable was set or undefined if it was not.

The yaws_api:getvar/2 function will call postvar/2 if the HTTP request is a HTTP POST and queryvar/2 if the request was a HTTP GET.

In some cases (including the upcoming Example 4-15) the data is sent to the server not as a set of name value pairs as from a HTML form, but as a JSON or XML object in the payload of a HTTP POST request. In this case the user data is in the clidata field of the #arg record. To extract this use code like in Example 4-1. This function takes the Arg#arg.clidata field and decodes the JSON into a data structure. It then logs the data, and finally it uses the rfc4627:get_field/3 function to extract a specific field from the data structure. (This was extracted from Example 4-14.)

Example 4-1. Getting a JSON from a HTTP POST

```
out(Arg) ->
    {ok, Json, _} = rfc4627:decode(Arg#arg.clidata),
    io:format("~n~p:~p POST request ~p~n",
        [?MODULE, ?LINE, Json]),
    Airport   = rfc4627:get_field(Json, "airport", <<>>),
    Airport.
```

If the user has uploaded a file with the mime type multipart/form-data, use the function yaws_api:parse_multipart_post/1. For more information, see Chapter 5.

Response and Headers

Another important part of REST is that HTTP status codes are used to return information to the client. So when creating a new airport record we should return a status of `201 Created`, not `200 OK`, and when a request is not successful because a resource does not exist the service should return `404 Not Found`. A complete list of HTTP status codes can be found at *http://www.w3.org/Protocols/rfc2616/rfc2616-sec10.html*.

By default Yaws will return a status of `200 OK`, so if some other status code is desired have the `out/1` function return `{status, Code}` with the desired HTTP code. The `out/1` function can return a list of tuples, so it is possible to set a status code, headers, and content (and any other options) from the return code. Table 4-1 shows a list of selected status codes.

Table 4-1. Selected status codes

Status Code	Description
100 Continue	Used when the client wants to send a large request; allows the server to accept or reject request based only on the headers. Client must send `Expect: 100-continue`.
200 OK	Standard HTTP response. The body should contain content.
201 Created	A new resource has been created.
202 Accepted	Request accepted, but not yet acted on.
203 Non Authoritative Information	Server processed the request but may lack a full response.
204 No Content	The server processed the request but is not returning any content.
205 Reset Content	Like 204, but the client must refresh its data.
206 Partial Content	The server is sending only a part of the data. This can be used to resume an interrupted download.
300 Multiple Choices	Server is presenting data in several formats; the client should choose one.
301 Moved Permanently	Redirect to new URI.
302 Found	Originally "Moved Temporarily"; should not be used in favor of 303 and 307.
303 See Other	Short-term redirection to a new URI.
304 Not Modified	Indicates that the client should use a cached copy of the resource.
307 Temporary Redirect	The resource is at a different URI on a temporary basis.
400 Bad Request	Request cannot be fulfilled due to bad syntax.
401 Unauthorized	The user must authenticate; this will prompt most browsers to ask for a username and password.
403 Forbidden	The server refused to respond to a request.
404 Not Found	Resource does not exist.
405 Method Not Allowed	Request used a HTTP verb not supported by a particular URI.
406 Not Acceptable	Server cannot generate content that matches the "Accept" headers. For example, an image may be available only as a .gif and the client wants it as a .png.

Status Code	Description
408 Request Timeout	Server timed out waiting for the client to send the request.
409 Conflict	Server cannot update resource due to a conflict, for example two users trying to update the same record.
410 Gone	Resource has been deleted and will not return. Ideally should be removed from search indexes, etc.
411 Length Required	Request must include the length of its content.
412 Precondition Failed	Request does not meet some precondition.
413 Request Entity Too Large	Could be used when a file to be uploaded is greater than the server wants to accept.
414 Request URI Too Long	The client sent a request URI that was too long.
417 Expectation Failed	Client sent an `Expect request-header` that the server cannot accept.
418 I'm a Little Teapot	Short and stout.
429 Too Many Requests	Used when one user is sending too many requests in a period of time.
500 Internal Server Error	Generic error message.
501 Not Implemented	Server cannot respond to the request method.
503 Service Unavailable	Server temporarily unavailable.

There are many options for how to build a frontend for testing. Obviously we could build a JavaScript application in a browser with jQuery and backbone.js or ExtJS. However, for testing we will just use the Unix curl binary, which allows us to issue commands from a command line or script.

To demonstrate this we will create a simple database listing airports. For each airport we will store a number of pieces of information including the airport name, the iata_code (e.g., "JFK"), the city and country where the airport is located, and a list of runways. The runways are stored in a runway record. These records are defined in Example 4-2.

Example 4-2. Airport record

```
-record(airport,
        {code, city, country, name }).
```

In any application where there is persistent data, a choice must be made as to how to store it. For this example we will use Erlang's built-in Mnesia data store. Mnesia is integrated with Erlang, so it will always be present when Erlang is present. It is also quite powerful and can do things like partition data across multiple servers and much more.

Mnesia is a rather flexible data store that mostly mirrors SQL features but is built into Erlang. However, Mnesia does not have the kind of constraints built into SQL nor the typing that SQL systems have. Mnesia also can be spread across several nodes. Mnesia tables can exist on disk or only in memory, which allows a lot of control over performance.

To find the HTTP method that was used, look in the `Arg` data structure (see Example 4-3). In this case we find the request structure `Rec`, and from there we look in the method field. This could in fact be done in one line, but is shown in two for clarity.

Example 4-3. Deriving the method

```
method(Arg) ->
  Rec = Arg#arg.req,
  Rec#http_request.method.
```

Building the Response

When a request comes into the `rest` module it is routed to the `out/1` function. This function uses the `method/1` function (Example 4-3) to find the HTTP method, and then routes things to the `handle/2` function. There are four versions of this function, one each for GET, POST, PUT, and DELETE. Erlang will match the parameter and call the correct function.

> The HTTP verb GET, POST, HEAD, etc., is set as an Erlang atom and not a string.

QLC stands for Query List Comprehension and is a set of macros that overload the meaning of list comprehensions in Erlang to allow them to be used as a Mnesia database query.[1] The general structure is `[ReturnedValue || Row <- mnesia:table(TableName), filters]`, so in the GET clause of Example 4-4 it is taking a list of all the records in the table "airport". This is similar to the SQL statement `SELECT * FROM airports`.

The code in Example 4-4 (taken from Example 4-14) shows how to use QLC to query the Mnesia data store, and then turn that data into a JSON of the form seen in Example 4-5, which can be sent to the browser. (How to create a JSON will be covered in "JSON" on page 47.)

Example 4-4. Generating the content

```
do(Q)->
    F = fun() ->
               qlc:e(Q)
    end,
    {atomic, Value} = mnesia:transaction(F),
    Value.
```

---

1. For those who have worked in .NET, this is similar to LINQ.

```
convert_to_json(Lines) ->
    Data = [{obj,
            [{airport, Line#airport.code},
             {city,    Line#airport.city},
             {country, Line#airport.country},
             {name,    Line#airport.name}]}
          || Line <- Lines],
    JsonData = {obj, [{data, Data}]},
    rfc4627:encode(JsonData).

handle('GET', _Arg) ->
    io:format("~n ~p:~p GET Request ~n", [?MODULE, ?LINE]),
    Records = do(qlc:q([X || X <- mnesia:table(airport)])),
    Json = convert_to_json( Records),
    io:format("~n ~p:~p GET Request Response ~p ~n", [?MODULE, ?LINE, Json]),
    {html, Json};
```

Example 4-5. Generating the content (pretty printed)

```
{
    "data": [
        {
            "airport": "BOS",
            "city": "Boston",
            "country": "US",
            "name": "Logan"
        },
        {
            "airport": "JFK",
            "city": "New York",
            "country": "US",
            "name": "John F Kennedy"
        }
    ]
}
```

In the case of the GET request we want to query the Mnesia database for all airports. (This is a limited example; obviously in a real application this would probably be filtered in some way.)

The GET clause of the handle/2 method calls the qlc:q function with a list comprehension that allows the function to retrieve the entire "airports" table. It would also be possible to filter this using guards if needed. This will return a list of records which is put into "Rec".

In many cases the format in which we want to return data to the client may be specified by the client. This could be done by using the HTTP Accept header. For example, an application could send an Accept header like the following:

```
Accept: application/xml, application/json
```

This client would like a response in XML or JSON format, but would probably prefer XML. Other clients may specify something else. In the case where a web service is being used to feed a JavaScript user interface, it is probably OK to ignore this and always return one data format. However, more and more web services are being used for computer-to-computer applications, and in this case it may be that being able to support multiple data formats is a key feature of an application design. It is also a good idea to return the content to the browser or other client with the correct MIME type. The choice of whether to allow multiple response formats will come down to the specifics of what is required of an application. However, in most cases picking one and sticking with it will be acceptable.

When choosing a response type, there are two possible ways that the code can decide. If the server would rather send one format it can query the headers out of the `Arg#arg.headers` data structure with a query that asks if a given format is allowed. One could imagine a function like Example 4-6 where a MIME type and `Arg` are passed in and it returns `true` or `false` if the MIME type is in the list. If the `Allowed` header is not present, the program should do something well defined. It should also be able to deal with a request that includes a format of */*, which indicates all formats are OK.

Example 4-6. Format allowed

```
requested_formats(Arg) ->
    Rec     = Arg#arg.headers,
    Accept = Rec#headers.accept,
    [AcceptFormats| _]  = string:tokens(Accept, ";"),
    string:tokens(AcceptFormats, ",").


accept_format(Format, Headers) ->
    Res = lists:any(fun (F) ->
                string:equal(Format, F)
            end, Headers).
```

JSON

One very common method of data exchange is JSON, which was created by Douglas Crockford from the Object Literal Syntax of JavaScript and is defined by RFC 4627. JSON is simple to read and there are JSON implementations for almost any language that may be needed, so it plays well with others.

Once Mnesia has given us a list of airports, we must convert that data to JSON format to transmit to the browser. To do this there are a number of Erlang modules that can be used to convert Erlang data to a JSON representation. These include the `rfc4627` module that can be found on GitHub, the `json2` module that is included with Yaws, and a bunch of others.

When decoding a JSON with the `rfc4627:decode/1` function, there are two options. The first is that it will return `{ok, Result, Remainder}`. In this case, `Result` is the decoded JSON and `Remainder` is any part of the input string that was not parsed. If for some reason `rfc4627:decode/1` cannot parse the JSON, it will return `{error, Reason}`. The most probable cause of this is a malformed JSON.

 If you are having problems with JSON format data, try passing it through JSONLint (*http://jsonlint.com*). This will validate JSON strings and pretty-print them as well.

Sometimes the client will send us a JSON; one problem here is that the name-value pair format of a JavaScript object represented in a JSON does not map very well onto Erlang's data structures. However, it is still possible to map a JSON object onto Erlang's data structures. Given the JSON in Example 4-7, the Erlang `rfc4627` module will map it onto a data structure as in Example 4-8.

Example 4-7. JSON object

```
{
    "cust_id": 123,
    "name": "Joe Armstrong",
    "note": "wrote Erlang"
}
```

Example 4-8. Decoded JSON object

```
{obj,[{"cust_id",123},
     {"name",<<"Joe Armstrong">>},
     {"note",<<"wrote Erlang">>}]}
```

The mapping of JSON data types onto Erlang types is something to keep in mind. Arrays in JSON map onto lists in Erlang. Numbers in JSON map onto numbers. String values as shown in Example 4-8 are mapped onto binary values in Erlang. However, there are a number of JSON encoders and decoders in Erlang, and not all of them will map a JSON onto exactly the same data structure.

 If you try to encode a PID value from Erlang into a JSON, it will not work and will give a rather confusing error message.

The object is mapped onto a data structure starting with the atom `obj` to mark it as a JSON object, then a set of name-value pairs as an array of two value tuples.

To get the value of a specific field from the JSON object use the `rfc4627:get_field/2` function, which will take the data structure put out by `decode/1` and the name of a field as an atom and return the value of that field. So calling `rfc4627:get_field(Obj, name)` on Example 4-8 will return `<<"Joe Armstrong">>`. In addition, there is a function `rfc4627:get_field/3` that works just like `rfc4627:get_field/2` except that the third parameter is a default value if the value is not set in the JSON.

When constructing an `obj` structure as in Example 4-8, the function `rfc4627:set_field/3` will be helpful. It will take an object of the form shown in the example and return a new object of the same type with a field set to a value. So calling `rfc4627:set_field(Obj, country, "Sweden")` on the example record will add the country to the data structure.

To create a JSON string to pass to a client, use the `rfc4627:encode/1` function, which will take data in the same format put out by `rfc4627:decode/1` and turn it back into a JSON data string. So the data structure in Example 4-8 will be encoded into a JSON that is equivalent to Example 4-7. The example here has been reformatted by JSONLint to be easier to read; the output will be all on one line.

It would be tempting to try to use code similar to Example 4-9 to convert a generic Erlang record to a JSON (or something that will be converted to a JSON). However, the access to fields in a record must be done with literal atoms, so `Rec#Type.Field` won't work. It must be done as `Rec#test_record.airport_name`. (It is possible to use macros here, however.)

Example 4-9. Convert to JSON (this won't work!)

```
-module(convert_to_json).

-record(test_record, {room_name, room_users, desc}).
-export([convert_to_json/2]).

convert_to_json(Type, Rec) ->
    Fields = record_info(fields, Type),
    Struct = [{Field, Rec#Type.Field} || Field <- Fields],
    {obj, Struct}.
```

XML

While our application uses JSON for data transfer, in some cases XML may be a better choice. So having a way to convert data from Erlang records to XML would be a useful thing.

XML can be generated in Yaws with the `ehtml` data type. The content `type1` should be set to `application/xml` and the top line should be set to a standard XML declaration similar to this:

```
<?xml version="1.0" encoding="utf-8"?>
```

Alternatively, a template engine like ErlyDTL (see "ErlyDTL" on page 26) can be used to make XML as in Example 2-20.

In addition to generating XML with the `ehtml` type, it is also possible to generate it with the `xmerl` package included with Erlang, and parse it with `xmerl_scan`.

It will also often be necessary to scan an existing XML document. This can be done with the `xmerl_scan` package that is included with Erlang. There are two basic functions to do this, `file/1` and `string/1`. The `file/1` function will take the path to a file on disk as a parameter, while `string/1` will take the XML in a string that is already in memory. There are also versions of both that allow the programmer to specify a number of options in a second parameter. Check the `xmerl_scan` man page for all the possible options.

The data structure that is created when you run `xmerl_scan:file/1` is rather long. For the XML shown in Example 4-10, it will generate data as shown in Example 4-11. To extract a specific element from this data structure it is possible to use XPATH via the `xmerl_xpath` module.

Example 4-10. Sample XML

```
<?xml version="1.0" encoding="utf-8"?>
<user>
  <id>31415926</id>
  <name>Joe Armstrong</name>
  <note>Created Erlang</note>
</user>
```

Example 4-11. Parsed XML

```
{{xmlElement,user,user,[],
             {xmlNamespace,[],[]},
             [],1,[],
             [{xmlText,[{user,1}],1,[],"\n   ",text},
              {xmlElement,id,id,[],
                          {xmlNamespace,[],[]},
                          [{user,1}],
                          2,[],
                          [{xmlText,[{id,2},{user,1}],1,[],"31415926",text}],
                          [],".",undeclared},
              {xmlText,[{user,1}],3,[],"\n   ",text},
              {xmlElement,name,name,[],
                          {xmlNamespace,[],[]},
                          [{user,1}],
                          4,[],
                          [{xmlText,[{name,4},{user,...}],1,[],[...],...}],
                          [],undefined,undeclared},
              {xmlText,[{user,1}],5,[],"\n   ",text},
              {xmlElement,note,note,[],
                          {xmlNamespace,[],[]},
                          [{user,1}],
                          6,[],
                          [{xmlText,[{...}|...],1,...}],
                          [],undefined,undeclared},
              {xmlText,[{user,1}],7,[],"\n",text}],
             [],".",undeclared},
 []}
```

Responding to the REST Request

When the user sends a POST request to the web server, that is the key to create a new airport record. The handler needs to find the airport name and other information from the POST content with yaws_api:postvar/2, and then should create a new airport with airport:create_airport/5. Example 4-12 takes the airport name and other information, creates an airport record, and inserts it into the Mnesia database. The nice thing about Mnesia is that if it is set up correctly, data will automatically be replicated across a cluster.

Normally, when responding to a HTTP request, we return a status of 200 OK. However, here we are creating a new resource, so returning a status of 201 Created makes sense. The body could be blank or contain any relevant information such as the name and ID of the airport. In this case we return the JSON that was sent by the browser, as the ExtJS framework expects that.

Example 4-12. Generating the content

```
handle('POST', Arg) ->
    {ok, Json, _} = rfc4627:decode(Arg#arg.clidata),
    io:format("~n~p:~p POST request ~p~n",
              [?MODULE, ?LINE, Json]),
    Airport  = rfc4627:get_field(Json, "airport", <<>>),
    City    = rfc4627:get_field(Json, "city", <<>>),
    Country  = rfc4627:get_field(Json, "country", <<>>),
    Name    = rfc4627:get_field(Json, "name", <<>>),
    _Status = addAirport(Airport, City, Country, Name),
    [{status, 201},
     {html, Arg#arg.clidata}];
```

A Full Example

So far this chapter has used little bits of code to show how to do different parts of a service. This section will take those bits and unify them into a complete service that can be used as a basis for your own applications. Most (but not all) of the code here is from the previous sections.

In general, a REST service will want to do one of two things: either work records in Mnesia or another data store, or interact with some form of backend application by sending messages back and forth. Here is a full example using Mnesia.

In this example, when a GET event comes in, it will query Mnesia, return a list of all the airports, and return them to the user.

When the user sends a POST request, the system will add a new record to the Mnesia data store. If needed we could also take other actions here, such as invalidating a cache or calling other functions to take other actions.

When the user sends a PUT request, we will update an existing record. In this case we will look it up by its IATA code and update the airport for new information. We cannot handle the case where an airport changes its IATA code, but this should be rare enough a case that we could delete the record and create it again.

When the user sends a DELETE request, we will delete the record from the data store.

There is also an extra clause at the end to catch any requests that are not one of the four major HTTP requests and return a "405 Method Not Allowed" response.

In order for all this to work, we need to have an airport data format; in this case it is very simple and shown in Example 4-2. This record includes only the airport IATA code, name, city, and country.

We must also set up a table in the Mnesia data store, as in Example 4-13. This must be done before the code is run and normally would be done in an *.erlang* file that Yaws will run on startup.

 The calls to io:format serialize all server activity through the IO server; remove them for production.

Example 4-13. Setting up Mnesia

```
%% Add this to the .erlang file
application:start(mnesia).
mnesia:create_table(airport,
            [
            {attributes,record_info(fields, airport)},
            {index, [country]}]).
```

Example 4-14 brings all of the airport example code together.

Example 4-14. Full airport example

```
-module(rest).
-include("/usr/lib/erlang/lib/stdlib-1.17.3/include/qlc.hrl").
-include("/usr/lib/yaws/include/yaws_api.hrl").
-export([out/1, addAirport/4, handle/2]).
%-compile(export_all).


-define(RECORD_TYPE,      airport).
-define(RECORD_KEY_FIELD, code).

-record(?RECORD_TYPE,
        {?RECORD_KEY_FIELD, city, country, name }).

out(Arg) ->
    Method = method(Arg) ,
    io:format("~p:~p ~p Request ~n", [?MODULE, ?LINE, Method]),
    handle(Method, Arg).
```

```erlang
method(Arg) ->
  Rec = Arg#arg.req,
  Rec#http_request.method.


convert_to_json(Lines) ->
    Data = [{obj,
          [{airport, Line#?RECORD_TYPE.code},
           {city,    Line#?RECORD_TYPE.city},
           {country, Line#?RECORD_TYPE.country},
           {name,    Line#?RECORD_TYPE.name}]}
        || Line <- Lines],
    JsonData = {obj, [{data, Data}]},
    rfc4627:encode(JsonData).

addAirport(Code, City, Country, Name) ->
    NewRec = #?RECORD_TYPE{
        ?RECORD_KEY_FIELD   = Code,
        city            = City,
        country         = Country,
        name            = Name},
    io:format("~p:~p Adding Airport ~p~n",
        [?MODULE,?LINE, NewRec]),
    Add = fun() ->
                        mnesia:write(NewRec)
                end,
    {atomic, _Rec} = mnesia:transaction(Add),
    NewRec.


handle('GET', _Arg) ->
    io:format("~n ~p:~p GET Request ~n", [?MODULE, ?LINE]),
    Records = do(qlc:q([X || X <- mnesia:table(?RECORD_TYPE)])),
    Json = convert_to_json( Records),
    io:format("~n ~p:~p GET Request Response ~p ~n", [?MODULE, ?LINE, Json]),
    {html, Json};

handle('POST', Arg) ->
    {ok, Json, _} = rfc4627:decode(Arg#arg.clidata),
    io:format("~n~p:~p POST request ~p~n",
            [?MODULE, ?LINE, Json]),
    Airport   = rfc4627:get_field(Json, "airport", <<>>),
    City    = rfc4627:get_field(Json, "city", <<>>),
    Country   = rfc4627:get_field(Json, "country", <<>>),
    Name    = rfc4627:get_field(Json, "name", <<>>),
    _Status = addAirport(Airport, City, Country, Name),
    [{status, 201},
     {html, Arg#arg.clidata}];


handle('PUT', Arg) ->
    [IndexValue,_] = string:tokens(Arg#arg.pathinfo),
    {ok, Json, _} = rfc4627:decode(Arg#arg.clidata),
    io:format("~p:~p PUT request ~p ~p~n",
```

```erlang
                [?MODULE, ?LINE, IndexValue, Json]),
    Airport   = rfc4627:get_field(Json, "airport", <<>>),
    City    = rfc4627:get_field(Json, "city", <<>>),
    Country   = rfc4627:get_field(Json, "country", <<>>),
    Name    = rfc4627:get_field(Json, "name", <<>>),

    NewRec = #?RECORD_TYPE{
        ?RECORD_KEY_FIELD    = Airport,
        city             = City,
        country          = Country,
        name             = Name},

    io:format("~p:~p Renaming ~p",
            [?MODULE, ?LINE, NewRec]),
    ChangeName = fun() ->
            mnesia:delete(
              {?RECORD_KEY_FIELD, IndexValue}),
                    mnesia:write(NewRec)
              end,
    {atomic, _Rec} = mnesia:transaction(ChangeName),
    [{status, 200},
     {html, IndexValue}];


handle('DELETE', Arg) ->

    [IndexValue, _ ] = string:tokens(Arg#arg.pathinfo),
    io:format("~p:~p DELETE request ~p",
            [?MODULE, ?LINE, IndexValue]),

    Delete = fun() ->
                    mnesia:delete(
                      {?RECORD_KEY_FIELD, IndexValue})
            end,

    Resp = mnesia:transaction(Delete),
    case Resp of
        {atomic, ok} ->
            [{status, 204}];
        {_, Error} ->
            io:format("~p:~p Error ~p ",
                    [?MODULE, ?LINE, Error]),
            [{status, 400},
             {html, Error}]
    end;


handle(Method,_) ->
    [{error, "Unknown method " ++ Method},
     {status, 405},
     {header, "Allow: GET, HEAD, POST, PUT, DELETE"}
     ].


do(Q)->
```

```erlang
    F = fun() ->
               qlc:e(Q)
    end,
    {atomic, Value} = mnesia:transaction(F),
    Value.
```

Finally, we need a frontend to use all this with. I created a simple frontend in Coffee-Script with Ext JS (see *http://sencha.com*) and it is included in Example 4-15. This creates a UI in the browser that looks like Figure 4-1.

Example 4-15. CoffeeScript frontend (airport.coffee)

```coffeescript
makeModel = ->
        Ext.define("Airport",
                extend: "Ext.data.Model",
                fields:[
                        {name: "airport"}
                        {name: "city"}
                        {name: "country"}
                        {name: "name"}
                        ]
        )

makeStore = ->
        model = makeModel()
        store = Ext.create("Ext.data.Store",
                autoLoad : true
                autoSync : true
                model    : model
                proxy    :
                        type   : "rest"
                        url    : "airports.yaws" # Will need to change the backend here
                        reader :
                                type: "json"
                                root: "data"
                        writer:
                                type: "json"
        )

setupAirports = ->
        store     = makeStore()
        rowEditing = Ext.create "Ext.grid.plugin.RowEditing"
        grid      = Ext.create "Ext.grid.Panel"
                renderTo : document.body
                plugins  : [rowEditing]
                width    : 500
                height   : 300
                title    : "Airports"
                store    : store
                columns:
                        [
                            {
                                        text     : 'Airport',
                                        width    : 60
                                        sortable : true
```

```
                              dataIndex : "airport"
                              editor    : {allowBlank: false}
                }
                {

                              text      : "City"
                              dataIndex : "city"
                              sortable  : true
                              editor    : {allowBlank: false}
                }
                {

                              text      : "Country"
                              dataIndex : "country"
                              sortable  : true
                              editor    : {allowBlank: false}
                }
                {

                              text      : "Airport Name"
                              dataIndex : "name"
                              sortable  : true
                              editor    : {allowBlank: false}
                }
          ]
      dockedItems:
          [

              xtype: "toolbar"
              items:
                  [
                      {

                              text: "Add"
                              handler: ->
                                  store.insert(0, new Airport())
                                      rowEditing.startEdit(0,0)
                      }
                      {

                              itemId: 'delete'
                              text: "Delete"
                              handler:  () ->
                                      selection = grid
                                          .getView()
                                          .getSelectionModel()
                                          .getSelection()[0]
                                      if(selection)
                                          store.remove(selection)
                      }
                  ]
          ]

Ext.onReady setupAirports
```

Figure 4-1. Airports UI in a browser

CHAPTER 5

File Upload

While being able to submit a form or other post variables via Ajax is a useful thing, sooner or later most applications will want to let a user upload a file, for example an avatar image or a video.

Yaws allows an application to receive a file from the user in the standard upload format that users of other server-side technologies such as PHP have come to expect.

When uploading a file in PHP, PHP buffers the input into the /tmp directory and then sends the finished file to your program. In Yaws, the server sends the file in chunks to your code. So instead of getting a complete file, the programmer has to be ready to get a stream of chunks of data. This does put a little more work onto the programmer, but it also allows the programmer to work with an incomplete upload if that is desired.

The examples in this chapter are taken from the example on the Yaws documentation website with a few minor changes. The full working code is in Example 5-4, while the examples preceding it show parts of the code for explanation.

To test uploading, you can of course use a browser, but using the curl[1] program from a command line makes everything easier to test. Using a command line like this one will upload a file from the local disk to the Yaws server. In this example, the file you specify should be copied to the upload directory, /tmp/YawsUploads—if that directory does not exist it will be created. When the upload is finished, the web server will return an HTML fragment with the text "File Upload Done".

```
curl -F radio=@large_audio_file.mp3 http://localhost:8081/upload.yaws
```

The File Upload Request

In the case of a file upload, out/1 will be called not just once but multiple times, with each call having a new slice of the data (see Example 5-1). In order to maintain the state

---

1. Curl is a standard Unix program and can be run in Windows with Cygwin.

of the upload (and anything else that may go along with it) Yaws provides a way to return a state from out/1 and have it returned to you in the next invocation. In this example, the state of the upload is encoded in the #upload{} record and stored between calls in Arg#arg.state.

The first clause in this function uses a guard to check if the Arg#arg.state field is not set. If it has not been set, then it creates a blank upload object and passes it to multipart/2. The second clause of the function simply gets the existing state object from Arg#arg.state and passes it to multipart/2.

Example 5-1. Repeated upload requests

```
<erl>
multipart(Arg, State) ->
    Parse = yaws_api:parse_multipart_post(Arg),
    case Parse of
        [] -> ok;
        {cont, Content, Res} ->
            case nextChunk(Arg, Res, State) of
                {done, Result} ->
                    Result;
                {cont, NewState} ->
                    {get_more, Content, NewState}
            end;
        {result, Res} ->
            case nextChunk(Arg, Res, State#upload{last=true}) of
                {done, Result} ->
                    Result;
                {cont, _} ->
                    err()
            end
    end.

out(A) when A#arg.state == undefined ->
    State = #upload{},
    multipart(A, State);
out(A) ->
    multipart(A, A#arg.state).
</erl>
```

The function yaws_api:parse_multipart_post/1 will return {result, Res} if this is the final chunk of data from the browser. However, if the function returns {cont, Contents, Res} then there is more data to come from the browser. At this point the out/1 function should return {get_more, Contents, State}. The next time out/1 is called, the State part of that tuple will be passed back in to be used as shown in Example 5-2.

When the upload is finished, multipart/2 will return a result such as {html, "Upload Finished"} that will be shown to the user. If the upload is not finished, it will return a tuple as described above to let Yaws know to give it more data. Note this example does not save the data that will be shown in "Saving to Disk" on page 61.

Example 5-2. Multipart

```
multipart(Arg, State) ->
    Parse = yaws_api:parse_multipart_post(Arg),
    case Parse of
        [] -> ok;
        {cont, Content, Res} ->
            case nextChunk(Arg, Res, State) of
                {done, Result}  >
                    Result;
                {cont, NewState} ->
                    {get_more, Content, NewState}
            end;
        {result, Res} ->
            case nextChunk(Arg, Res, State#upload{last=true}) of
                {done, Result} ->
                    Result;
                {cont, _} ->
                    err()
            end
    end.
```

Saving to Disk

The most obvious thing to do with a file upload is to save it to the filesystem. This may
be a final location for the file, or a way to buffer large uploads until they are finished
and can be pushed into some other storage mechanism so as not to use up large amounts
of memory.

To write a file to disk call the BIF `file:open/2` as in Example 5-3. If there is not an error,
this will return `{ok, FD}` where FD is the file handle that can be used to write to the file.
For full details on handling files in Erlang, see the Erlang manual pages.

Once the file has been opened, each subsequent chunk of data can be added to the file
with `file:write/2` until the end of the file, when `file:close/2` can be called to close
the file handle.

> If a process dies in the middle of writing a file, Erlang will close the file
> handle automatically. It may be worth it to have the monitoring mech-
> anism delete the file as well.

There are several clauses of the `writeToDisk/3` function in Example 5-3, but they all
take the same three parameters. The first is the standard `Arg` record that Yaws sends to
`out/1`, which is passed on here. The second is a list of the parts of the file to be saved,
and the third is the current state record.

The parts buffer is a list of chunks of the uploaded file that can be saved to disk. If the
list is empty and `State#upload.last` is false, then all the data that has been buffered has

been processed. In this case writeToDisk/3 will return {cont, State}, which will let Yaws know to send the next chunk of data when it arrives and wait until that happens.

When the buffer is not empty, it will consist of a list of tuples of the form {Atom, Data}. There are several possible atoms that could be sent.

The first element to be sent will be sent with the form {head, {Name, Options} }. To handle this, writeToDisk/3 should open the file handle, set up the state record, and then recursively call writeToDisk/3 with the new state record and the tail of the buffer list.

In the case of a chunk of data in the middle of a file, the head of the buffer will look like {body, Data}. In this case, the data should be written out to disk, and then write ToDisk/3 should again be called recursively with the tail of the list.

If the buffer list is empty and State#upload.last is true, then the file is finished uploading. At this point we can call file:close/1 to close the file handle. After that we can call upload_callback/1 to handle any operations that we may wish to handle after the upload finishes (such as syncing to other nodes or uploading to CouchDB) and we return a done status.

Example 5-3. Save file upload

```
writeToDisk(A, [{part_body, Data}|Res], State) ->
    writeToDisk(A, [{body, Data}|Res], State);

writeToDisk(_A, [], State) when State#upload.last==true,
                                State#upload.filename /= undefined,
                                State#upload.fd /= undefined ->
    file:close(State#upload.fd),
    upload_callback(State),
    Res= {html, "Done"},
    {done, Res};

writeToDisk(A, [], State) when State#upload.last==true ->
    {done, err()};

writeToDisk(_A, [], State) ->
    {cont, State};


writeToDisk(A, [{head, {_Name, Opts}}|Res], State ) ->
    case lists:keysearch(filename, 1, Opts) of
        {value, {_, Fname0}} ->
            Fname = yaws_api:sanitize_file_name(basename(Fname0)),
        TargetDir = "/tmp",
        file:make_dir(TargetDir),
        case file:open([TargetDir, Fname] ,[write]) of
        {ok, Fd} ->
            S2 = State#upload{filename = Fname,
                    fd = Fd},
            writeToDisk(A, Res, S2);
        Err ->
            {done, err()}
```

```
        end;
    false ->
            writeToDisk(A,Res,State)
    end;


writeToDisk(A, [{body, Data}|Res], State)
  when State#upload.filename /= undefined ->
    case file:write(State#upload.fd, Data) of
        ok ->
            writeToDisk(A, Res, State);
        Err ->
            {done, err()}
    end.
```

If uploading files is a large part of an application, then the disk can become a bottleneck in the application's performance. While the server may have 20 or 40 cores, the disk is very sequential and the slowest part of the system. This has to be considered in light of Amdahl's law (see "Amdahl's law" on page 8). It's possible that using something like Amazon's S3 might be a better solution (see "Saving to Amazon S3" on page 66).

Putting It All Together

Example 5-4 brings together the various pieces of code to show you how to upload a file in Yaws.

Example 5-4. Complete upload code (upload.yaws)

```
<erl>

-record(upload, {
        fd,
        filename,
        last}).

-define(DIR, "/tmp/").

out(Arg) when Arg#arg.state == undefined ->
    State = #upload{},
    multipart(Arg, State);
out(Arg) ->
    multipart(Arg, Arg#arg.state).

err() ->
    {ehtml,
     {p, [], "error"}}.

multipart(Arg, State) ->
    Parse = yaws_api:parse_multipart_post(Arg),
    case Parse of
        [] -> ok;
```

```
            {cont, Cont, Res} ->
                case addFileChunk(Arg, Res, State) of
                    {done, Result} ->
                        Result;
                    {cont, NewState} ->
                        {get_more, Cont, NewState}
                end;
            {result, Res} ->
                case addFileChunk(Arg, Res, State#upload{last=true}) of
                    {done, Result} ->
                        Result;
                    {cont, _} ->
                        err()
                end
    end.

addFileChunk(Arg, [{part_body, Data}|Res], State) ->
    addFileChunk(Arg, [{body, Data}|Res], State);

addFileChunk(_Arg, [], State) when State#upload.last     == true,
                                   State#upload.filename    /= undefined,
                                   State#upload.fd    /= undefined ->

    file:close(State#upload.fd),
    Res = {ehtml,
           {p,[], "File upload done"}},
    {done, Res};

addFileChunk(Arg, [], State) when State#upload.last==true ->
    {done, err()};

addFileChunk(_Arg, [], State) ->
    {cont, State};

addFileChunk(Arg, [{head, {_Name, Opts}}|Res], State ) ->
    case lists:keysearch(filename, 1, Opts) of
        {value, {_, Fname0}} ->
            Fname = yaws_api:sanitize_file_name(basename(Fname0)),

            %% we must not put the file in the
            %% docroot, it may execute uploade code if the
            %% file is a .yaws file !!!!!
            file:make_dir(?DIR),
            case file:open([?DIR, Fname] ,[write]) of
            {ok, Fd} ->
                S2 = State#upload{filename = Fname,
                            fd = Fd},
                addFileChunk(Arg, Res, S2);
            Err ->
                {done, err()}
            end;
        false ->
                addFileChunk(Arg,Res,State)
    end;
```

```
addFileChunk(Arg, [{body, Data}|Res], State)
  when State#upload.filename /= undefined ->
    case file:write(State#upload.fd, Data) of
        ok ->
            addFileChunk(Arg, Res, State);
        Err ->
            {done, err()}
    end.


basename(FilePath) ->
    case string:rchr(FilePath, $\\) of
        0 ->
            %% probably not a DOS name
            filename:basename(FilePath);
        N ->
            %% probably a DOS name, remove everything after last \
            basename(string:substr(FilePath, N+1))
    end.
</erl>
```

Storage in a Distributed System

The other complication is that writing the file to disk is probably not the correct way to handle the data. Erlang applications are distributed applications that run across a large number of servers. So if you upload a file from a user and it gets put on one node, it will not be seen by all the others. In this case it is a much better idea to keep the file in some sort of data store that has a way of replicating data around the network.

One solution is to try to put files on a shared filesystem. Unless it's a system like Amazon's S3, however, this can be a bad idea for a few reasons. First of all, the server that holds that system will become a bottleneck and a single point of failure. If that system were to go offline, the entire system will become unavailable. In addition, such a system would have to be quite large to handle the load of all the clients. Once again, the specifics of storage will have to be evaluated in light of the design and use of the application.

Using something like CouchDB (see "CouchDB" on page 12) would make sense here as it will allow the file to be propagated around the nodes of the application pretty well. In this case, what would probably happen is that the file would be uploaded to the local disk and then, when the upload is complete, it would be moved into the distributed system, be that CouchDB, Riak, HBase, or something else. This way, if a file upload is canceled or is corrupt, it will not be propagated out onto the network.

The other option for dealing with uploaded data is not to write it out at all, but to stream it to the users. Yaws is fully able to stream multimedia—see the Yaws documentation for more detail.

Saving to Amazon S3

Often we will want to take a file that a user has uploaded and make it available to the world to download. For example, think of a video on YouTube: the user uploads the file, probably does some manipulation of the data itself (converting formats, etc.), and then puts it somewhere that other users can view it.

One of the easiest ways to do this is to save the file to Amazon S3, a highly reliable cloud service that was built to solve this particular problem.

To use Amazon Web Services (AWS) from Erlang, use the erlcloud package at *https://github.com/gleber/erlcloud*. This package provides an Erlang interface to AWS. In this case we're interested only in the S3 service.

In Amazon S3 files live in buckets, and the code in Example 5-5 assumes that we have created a bucket already. The name of the bucket should be set by the -define() in the file. It is also possible to set default options on the bucket so that they are what your application needs. In addition, there are two keys that have to be set in this file (set them to your AWS keys).

Once the file has been uploaded from the user we need to upload it to S3 using the function erlcloud_s3:put_object/6 (if you want to allow default options there are also functions erlcloud_s3:put_object/3-5). Pass this function the bucket name, the key, and the value to upload; you can also pass options, HTTP headers, and a config object. This will upload the object to Amazon S3.

Once everything is set, we can upload a file to S3. To do this we pass in the key and value to the function s3:upload(), which will call erlcloud_s3:put_object/3 to upload the file.

If the file is on disk use the function s3:upload_file/2, which will automatically read the file into memory and pass it on to upload/2.

Example 5-5. Uploading to S3 (s3.erl)

```
-module(s3).

-define('ACCESS_KEY',        "********************").
-define('SECRET_ACCESS_KEY', "**************************************").
-define('BUCKET',            "*************").

-export([upload/2, upload_file/2]).

upload_file(Key, Path) ->
    {ok, Binary} = file:read_file(Path),
    upload(Key, Binary).


upload(Key, Value) ->
    erlcloud_ec2:configure(?ACCESS_KEY, ?SECRET_ACCESS_KEY),
    error_logger:info_msg("~p:~p Settng up AWS to S3 ~n",
```

```
                    [?MODULE, ?LINE]),
    R = erlcloud_s3:put_object(?BUCKET, Key, Value, [], [{"Content-type", "image/jpeg"}]),
    error_logger:info_msg("~p:~p Uploaded File ~p to S3 ~n",
                    [?MODULE, ?LINE, R]),
    {ok, R}.
```

Obviously, before using this example you will need to fill in your access key and secret key as well as the name of your bucket. In addition, before trying to upload code to S3 you will need to start up the **inets** and **ssl** services in Erlang. To do that, run these two lines when starting the Erlang node:

```
    inets:start().
    ssl:start().
```

To see this in action you can run Example 5-6, which will take a key and file from a Unix command line and upload it to S3. There are better AWS command-line tools, but this is a helpful way of testing the code in Example 5-5.

Example 5-6. Uploading to S3 shell wrapper (s3_upload)

```
#!/usr/bin/env escript
-export([main/1]).

main([Key, File_Name]) ->
    inets:start(),
    ssl:start(),
    s3:upload_file(Key, File_Name).
```

CHAPTER 6

WebSockets

Traditionally HTTP is not very good for live communications. The communication stream is controlled by the client and is really designed for the case where the client wants to load or set data from time to time. A number of methods have been used to simulate TCP-socket-like behavior over HTTP but none of them works very well. HTML5 introduced the idea of WebSockets, a full-on, bi-directional communication channel between the browser and a server.

In some ways WebSockets take the opposite approach to dealing with interactions between the browser and the client than REST does. REST is built around the idea that the browser (or other client) will send a number of discrete requests to the server of the form, show this data, or perform some action.

 As WebSockets are not supported in all browsers, having a cross-platform way of handling communication would be helpful. This can be done with the JavaScript package Socket.io (*http://socket.io*) and the Erlang package socket.io-erlang (*https://github.com/yrashk/socket .io-erlang*).

From an Erlang perspective, WebSockets make interactions between the browser and Erlang applications more transparent. An Erlang application will generally consist of a bunch of little servers passing messages around between them. When opening up WebSockets between the user's browser and the Erlang application, we can push that model out onto the user's browser.

To visualize this, look at Figure 6-1. Here the Erlang cloud on the left consists of a bunch of processes (shown as squares) passing messages between them (shown as arrows). There is one process shown in orange with rounded corners holding open the WebSocket (the double arrow), which is talking to the web browser and the client-side application. By extension there could be many sockets connecting to many web browsers allowing communications between the users.

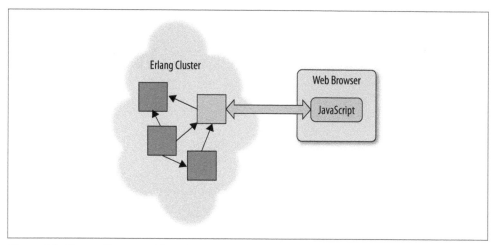

Figure 6-1. Cluster diagram with sockets

Thankfully, while the syntax of how events handlers are called in JavaScript and Erlang is somewhat different, the semantics are pretty similar. In Erlang we can use a `receive` block or an OTP behavior like `gen_server` or `gen_fsm`. In JavaScript we can use the `.onmessage` event handler and find the data in a dictionary in the parameter list.

However, the web browser does not understand the Erlang message format, so we will need to translate between the internal messages being sent around by Erlang and a format that the browser can understand. This can be done with JSON, XML, HTML, or a custom format. In this chapter, I will use JSON because it is the easiest to work with in the browser, but other formats can work too if they make sense.

The WebSocket Request

To set up a WebSocket in JavaScript with jQuery, use code as in Example 6-1. The socket will be opened by creating a `WebSocket` object with the URL of the server resource. Once the socket is ready for action, JavaScript will call the `socket.onopen` handler function.

Example 6-1. socket.js

```
$(function ()
{
    var WebSocket = window.WebSocket || window.MozWebSocket;
    var socket = new WebSocket("ws://localhost:8081/websockets/basic_echo_callback.yaws");

    // wait for socket to open
    socket.onopen = function ()
    {

        $('input#echo').on('keypress', function (event)
                          {
```

```
                    if ( event.which == 13 ) {
                        event.preventDefault();
                        var msg = $(this).val();

                        socket.send(JSON.stringify(
                            {
                                message:msg
                            }));
                    }
                });

        socket.onmessage = function (msg)
        {
            var message = $.parseJSON(msg.data);
            var html    = $('div#messages').html() + message.message  + "<br>\n";
            $('div#messages').html(html);

        }
    }
});
```

As with much of HTML5, not all browsers support WebSockets. As of this writing, the WebSocket interface is supported by Google Chrome and Mozilla Firefox, and Microsoft has said that WebSockets will be a feature of Internet Explorer Version 10. Safari, Opera, and the mobile browsers do not yet fully support WebSockets. (Opera actually does support them but only if you explicitly turn them on, which most users probably don't.) The Mobile Safari (iOS) and Android browsers also do not fully support WebSockets. There is also a plug-in for PhoneGap to allow WebSockets to be used on that platform.

WebSockets are new technology and the specifications for them have changed a few times, so they should be used with caution at the moment. I hope that within a few years we will be able to use them more fully. The Yaws team has been doing a pretty good job of keeping up to date with the changes, so as long as you keep Yaws up to date you should be OK.

The JavaScript interface to sockets, then, contains two main functions: a way to send messages to the server, and a way to handle messages that come back. To send a message, use the function socket.send(), which will send a string to the server. In this case it is the content of the input box, and is triggered when the input box receives a change event.

To handle incoming messages, use the socket.onmessage handler, which gets called when the server sends us a message.

Now that we have explored (in brief) the JavaScript interface to how to build a web socket, it is time to move on to the server side. When the browser opens up a web socket, it sends a request to the server that looks like a standard HTTP request but with the addition of an Upgrade header, as in Example 6-2.

Example 6-2. Upgrade header

```
Upgrade: WebSocket
```

This header can be found with the `is_websocket/1` function, as shown in Example 6-3. This will return true if the request is to open a socket and false otherwise.

Example 6-3. Get upgrade header

```
is_websocket(#headers{other=L}) ->
    lists:foldl(fun({http_header,_,K0,_,V}, false) ->
                    K = case is_atom(K0) of
                            true ->
                                atom_to_list(K0);
                            false ->
                                K0
                        end,
                    case string:to_lower(K) of
                        "upgrade" ->
                            true;
                        _ ->
                            false
                    end;
                (_, Acc) ->
                    Acc
            end, false, L).
```

Basic WebSocket Handler

The main conceptual difference between a WebSocket and a normal HTTP connection is that an HTTP connection is a one-shot item. The request comes in, the server does something and sends back a response, and that is the end of it. With a socket, the connection is much more like a persistent TCP socket connection, where multiple pieces of data are sent back and forth over an extended period of time, as long as several hours in some cases.[1]

 TheYaws WebSockets interfaces have changed recently. This chapter works with Yaws Version 1.92, which was released December 23, 2011; future versions may change things again.

To deal with a WebSocket, a callback module should be defined that exports a function `handle_message/1` (there is also an advanced mode that uses `handle_message/2`). This function will be called by Yaws each time the browser sends data over the socket.

If there is no need for the function to save some form of state from one call to the next, you will need to invoke your socket in advanced mode and do a bit more work to save

---

1. Technically HTTP also exists over a socket, but it is a short-lived one that is closed as soon as the request is done, and does not take advantage of much of the power of TCP sockets.

up partial frames. In that case handle_message/1 should be replaced by handle_message/2, which has a bunch more options.

The handle_message/1 function should take as an option a tuple in the form {Type, Data} where Type can be text or binary and Data is the message that is sent. In Example 6-4 (which was taken from the Yaws sources) there are several clauses that show some of the different cases that can occur.

Example 6-4. handle_message/1

```
-module(basic_echo_callback).

%% Export for websocket callbacks
-export([handle_message/1, say_hi/1]).


handle_message({text, Message}) ->
    io:format("~p:~p basic echo handler got ~p~n",
        [?MODULE, ?LINE, Message]),
    {reply, {text, <<Message/binary>>}}.

say_hi(Pid) ->
    io:format("asynchronous greeting~n", []),
    yaws_api:websocket_send(Pid, {text, <<"hi there!">>}).
```

When handle_message/1 is called it can return one of three responses. If it wishes to reply to the incoming message, it should return {reply, {Type, Data}}, which will send that message back out to the client.

If handle_message/1 does not have any message to send back, it should return the atom noreply.

If the server needs to send data to the client not in response to an action by the client, which is after all one of the main reasons to use a WebSocket, the function yaws_api:websocket_end/2 as shown in the function say_hi/1 in Example 6-4 will allow that message to be sent. This can be used in a standard receive loop to allow data from other parts of an application to be sent to the client.

When the request to establish a WebSocket first arrives to the out/1 function, return {websocket, CallBackModule, Options} where CallBackModule is the module with handle_message/1,2 defined and Options are any initial state that should be passed in (often just an empty list). A full Erlang implementation of the WebSocket setup code is shown in Example 6-5. This brings together pieces shown previously for a full picture.

Example 6-5. Setting up a WebSocket

```
<erl>

get_upgrade_header(#headers{other=L}) ->
    lists:foldl(fun({http_header,_,K0,_,V}, undefined) ->
                    K = case is_atom(K0) of
                            true ->
```

```
                                atom_to_list(KO);
                            false ->
                                    KO
                        end,
                    case string:to_lower(K) of
                        "upgrade" ->
                                true;
                        _ ->
                                false
                    end;
                (_, Acc) ->
                        Acc
            end, undefined, L).


%%-----------------------------------------------------------------------------
out(Arg) ->
    case get_upgrade_header(Arg#arg.headers) of
    true ->
        error_logger:warning_msg("Not a web socket client~n"),
        {content, "text/plain", "You're not a web sockets client! Go away!"};
    false ->
        error_logger:info_msg("Starting web socket~n"),
        {websocket, basic_echo_callback, []}
    end.

</erl>
```

To close the connection to the client, handle_message/1 can return {close, Reason}.

This echo code in action will look like Figure 6-2. When the browser sends data to the server, this code is set up to log it as shown in Example 6-6.

Example 6-6. Log from a WebSocket

```
=INFO REPORT==== 13-Mar-2012::16:43:25 ===
Starting web socket
basic_echo_callback:10 basic echo handler got <<"{\"message\":\"This is a Test\"}">>
```

Advanced WebSocket Handler

If a process needs more control over the WebSockets or needs to maintain state, using handle_message/2 will allow the programmer to do that. Contrast the implementation of handle_message/2 in Example 6-7 with that of handle_message/1 in Example 6-4. In Example 6-7 the first parameter is a #ws_frame_info record versus the tuple above. This lets the programmer work with partial frames. The downside is that you must handle both the state and the partial frames yourself. If being able to handle partial frames is not something you need, then some form of abstraction could be created to manage that and just expose the state handling features.

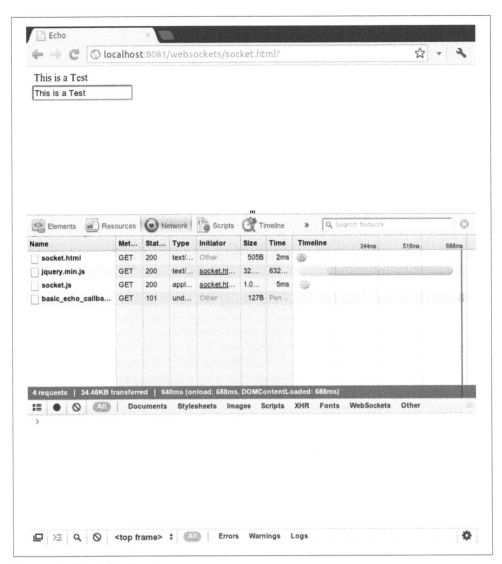

Figure 6-2. WebSockets in action

Example 6-7. Advanced WebSocket interface

```
%%%==============================================================
%%% compiled using erlc -I include src/advanced_echo_callback.erl
%%%==============================================================

-module(advanced_echo_callback).

-export([handle_message/2]).

-include("yaws_api.hrl").
```

```erlang
%% define callback state to accumulate a fragmented WS message
%% which we echo back when all fragments are in, returning to
%% initial state.
-record(state, {frag_type = none,            % fragment type
                acc = <<>>}).                % accumulate fragment data

%% start of a fragmented message
handle_message(#ws_frame_info{fin=0,
                              opcode=FragType,
                              data=Data},
               #state{frag_type=none, acc = <<>>}) ->
    {noreply, #state{frag_type=FragType, acc=Data}};

%% non-final continuation of a fragmented message
handle_message(#ws_frame_info{fin=0,
                 opcode=continuation,
                              data=Data},
               #state{frag_type = FragType, acc = Acc}) ->
    {noreply, #state{frag_type=FragType, acc = <<Acc/binary,Data/binary>>}};

%% end of text fragmented message
handle_message(#ws_frame_info{fin=1,
                              opcode=continuation,
                              data=Data},
               #state{frag_type=text, acc=Acc}) ->
    Unfragged = <<Acc/binary, Data/binary>>,
    {reply, {text, Unfragged}, #state{frag_type=none, acc = <<>>}};

%% one full non-fragmented message
handle_message(#ws_frame_info{opcode=text, data=Data}, State) ->
    {reply, {text, Data}, State};

%% end of binary fragmented message
handle_message(#ws_frame_info{fin=1,
                              opcode=continuation,
                              data=Data},
               #state{frag_type=binary, acc=Acc}) ->
    Unfragged = <<Acc/binary, Data/binary>>,
    io:format("echoing back binary message~n",[]),
    {reply, {binary, Unfragged}, #state{frag_type=none, acc = <<>>}};

%% one full non-fragmented binary message
handle_message(#ws_frame_info{opcode=binary,
                              data=Data},
               State) ->
    io:format("echoing back binary message~n",[]),
    {reply, {binary, Data}, State};

handle_message(#ws_frame_info{opcode=ping,
                              data=Data},
               State) ->
    io:format("replying pong to ping~n",[]),
    {reply, {pong, Data}, State};

handle_message(#ws_frame_info{opcode=pong}, State) ->
```

```
%% A response to an unsolicited pong frame is not expected.
%% http://tools.ietf.org/html/\
%%              draft-ietf-hybi-thewebsocketprotocol-08#section-4
io:format("ignoring unsolicited pong~n",[]),
{noreply, State};

handle_message(#ws_frame_info{}=FrameInfo, State) ->
    io:format("WS Endpoint Unhandled message: ~p~n~p~n", [FrameInfo, State]),
    {close, {error, {unhandled message, FrameInfo}}}.
```

In addition, each time handle_message/2 is called in Example 6-7, it is also given a #state record. This state can then be kept across calls and updated as needed. Thus handle_message/2 should return {reply, {Type,Data}, State} or {noreply, State}, as opposed to the forms for handle_message/1 that do not include the State record. [2]

To signify that the advanced mode should be used instead of the basic mode, the out/1 function should return the tuple {websocket, Module, {advanced, InitialState}}.

---

2. This is very similar to how the OTP gen_server behavior works.

CHAPTER 7

Streaming

Sometimes you want to stream data from a server to a client, for example, for an Internet radio station or a service like Pandora or Ustream. Yaws can do this quite well and with minimal effort on the part of the programmer.

The difference between streamed data and a standard HTTP connection is that a stream can remain open for a long period of time (oftentimes hours or days) and send data to the client for that entire time. However, unlike WebSockets (see Chapter 6) a stream is a one-way data connection and will normally be binary data like music or video as opposed to textual data in a WebSocket.

Simple Streaming

To set up streaming in Yaws, the `out/1` function should return the tuple `{streamcontent, MimeType, FirstChunk}` as in Example 7-1.

Example 7-1. Setting up streaming (stream.yaws)

```
<erl>
 out(A) ->
    io:format("~nStarting audio stream~n"),
    spawn(streaming, stream_data, [self()]),
    {streamcontent, "audio/mp3", <<>>}.
</erl>
```

You must also spawn a new process to actually send the data to the client. This is done in Example 7-1 with the call to `spawn/3`. This will create a new process and pass the process ID of the creating process, as shown in Example 7-2. When creating that process, the `out/1` function passes its own PID via the `self/0` function to the function `streaming:stream_data/1`.

To actually send the data to the stream, call the function `yaws_api:stream_chunk_deliver/2` with the Yaws creating PID and the data to be sent. When the stream is finished, call `yaws_api:stream_chunk_end/1` to tell Yaws to close things down.

When streaming audio or video to the HTML5 `<audio>` and `<video>` tags, not all browsers support all formats. So it will be necessary to convert formats so that all users can see the content if your frontend is HTML5.

If the source of the data is faster than what is receiving the data, replace `yaws_api:stream_chunk_deliver/2` with `yaws_api_stream_chunk_deliver_blocking/2`. This will make sure that the data being sent does not overflow the client's buffers.

Example 7-2. Sending data to a stream (streaming.erl)

```erlang
-module(streaming).

-export([stream_data/1]).

stream_data(Pid) ->
    File    = "audio.mp3",
    FileHDL = open_file(File),
    stream_from_file(Pid, FileHDL, 1).

open_file(File) ->
    {ok, IoDevice} = file:open(File,
                    [read, binary]),
    IoDevice.

stream_from_file(Pid, File, I) ->
    Result = file:read(File, 4096),
    case Result of
    {ok, Data} ->
        yaws_api:stream_chunk_deliver_blocking(Pid,Data),
        stream_from_file(Pid, File, I+1);
    eof ->
        yaws_api:stream_chunk_end(Pid);
    {error,Reason}->
        error_logger:error_msg("~p:~p Error ~p ~n",
                    [?MODULE, ?LINE, Reason])
    end.
```

Of course, not all audio streams have to be played via a web browser. It is possible to play audio via a media player like Windows Media Player, iTunes, or VLC. Figure 7-1 shows an audio stream playing in VLC streamed from Yaws; the code is shown in Example 7-2.

While this example pulls data from the disk to send to a user for simplicity, it is also possible to have the data sent from another process that is receiving data from an external source. In that case, you want to change the function `stream_from_file/3` in Example 7-2 to a function that will have a receive block that will get the data.

The great advantage of this is that if you are sending data to a lot of receivers, it is possible to reduce the memory usage by having one receive loop handle a group of users. This would make a great deal of sense when data is streaming into an application in some way (say from an audio input).

Figure 7-1. VLC playing a stream from Yaws

In order to help visualize the flow of data in this application, take a look at Figure 7-2. In this diagram, data always moves from left to right. Data enters into the system via the left-most arrow and flows to the line of boxes in the Erlang cloud, which is a buffer that will send the data out to the streaming processes of the Clients.

 When sending large binary messages between processes, Erlang will not make a copy of the binary but just pass a reference. However, this is inadvisable to the user.

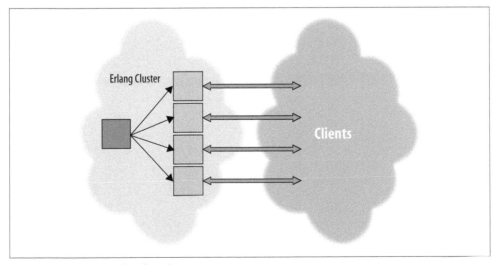

Figure 7-2. Streaming dataflow diagram

CHAPTER 8

Using the HTTP Client

Sometimes you need not to create an HTTP service but to consume one—perhaps to use a RESTful service or other API, or to load-test a server by hitting it with lots of requests at once. Erlang provides an HTTP client API that lets you do this. You can find the manual page for this module at *http://www.erlang.org/doc/man/httpc.html*. The httpc module is part of the standard Erlang distribution and does not have to be installed separately.

The first thing to do before using the httpc module is to start the inets service by calling inets:start() or application:start(inets). If you are running an application this can be done from the *.erlang* file or from the command line in testing. If you do not start inets, httpc will not work correctly. [1]

If there are some options that must be set for all calls then you can use the function httpc:set_options/1 or httpc:set_options/2. There are a number of options that can be set here, including all of the standard ones you would expect. Of particular note is the max_sessions option, which defaults to 2. In addition, if you need to set a proxy server you can do it here with the Proxy option. When calling set_option it will return ok or {error, Reason}.

 There are several other HTTP client packages for Erlang that provide more features, including ibrowse and lhttpc. You can find both online.

Making a Request

There are four functions available to make an HTTP request that run from one to five parameters (there is no function with three). These provide progressively more control over the HTTP request.

---

1. The inets service is a part of the standard Erlang distribution.

The simplest version of an HTTP request is `httpc:request/1`, which takes a URL as an argument. The `request/1` function simply performs an HTTP GET operation on the supplied URL as shown in Example 8-1. In this case a request to `http://www.goo gle.com` returns `{ok, Response}` or `{error, Reason}`. The `Response` will be the headers of the HTTP request along with the body of the request (truncated in Example 8-1).[2] If you wish to extract the values from a successful request you can use this line to extract the variables: `{ok, {{Version, 200, ReasonPhrase}, Headers, Body}}`.

Example 8-1. A simple HTTP request

```
14> httpc:request("http://www.google.com").
{ok,{{"HTTP/1.1",200,"OK"},
    [{"cache-control","private, max-age=0"},
     {"date","Tue, 24 Apr 2012 17:59:10 GMT"},
     {"server","gws"},
     {"content-length","40887"},
     {"content-type","text/html; charset=windows-1255"},
     {"expires","-1"},
     {"x-xss-protection","1; mode=block"},
     {"x-frame-options","SAMEORIGIN"}],
    "<!doctype html>..."}}
```

Sometimes a simple GET is not enough control—for example, you wish to access a REST service where you may need to send data with POST, PUT, or DELETE, or to test for the existence of a resource with a HEAD request.

To have more control over the request, use `request/4` or `request/5`. The first parameter here will be the HTTP verb set as an atom. Next will be the content of the request, followed by HTTP options, general options, and finally a profile parameter. (For a full list of options, see the manual page.)

To post data to a service, use the `request/4` version of the function as shown in Example 8-2. In this case we are sending a simple payload of data to the server, which can be URL-encoded or a JSON. In this example the payload is the data to be sent to the server and the URL is the address of the resource to send it to.

Example 8-2. HTTP post

```
-module(post).
-export([post/3]).

post(url_encoding, URL, Payload) ->
    httpc:request(post, {URL,
            [],
            "application/x-www-form-urlencoded",
            Payload},
        [],
        []);
post(json, URL, Payload) ->
```

---

2. I also removed several long lines here to make this example more readable.

```
httpc:request(post, {URL,
        [],
        "application/json",
        Payload},
    [],
    []).
```

If you do not want to have your process wait for the HTTP request for some reason, you could wrap the request in a fun and use spawn/1 to run it in its own process. However, the http:request/4 function will do this for you if it is passed [{sync, false}] as an option. In this case the request will return immediately and you will get the content in a receive block. The process will be sent the message {http, {RequestId, Result}}. This would be especially useful in the case where a program has to poll several servers for some information and collate the results. If you are used to doing Ajax in JavaScript this will feel familiar.

```
-module('async_request').
-export([async_request/1]).
async_request(URL) ->
    {ok, RequestId} =
    httpc:request(get, {URL, []}, [], [{sync, false}]),
    receive
    {http, {RequestId, Result}} ->
        Result
    after 500 ->
        error
    end.
```

Finally, if the HTTP request will return a large amount of data, it may be useful to have it written to disk for further processing. To do this you can use the option {stream, Filename} as in Example 8-3. In this case, the request/4 function will return {ok, saved_to_file} or {error, Reason} depending on what happened. It is also possible to stream data to a process by passing self or {self, once} instead of a filename. For more details on how that works, look at the httpc man page on *http://erlang.org*.

Example 8-3. Save to a file (stream_to.erl)

```
-module('stream_to').
-export([stream_to/2]).


stream_to(URL, Filename) ->
    httpc:request(get,
        {URL,[]},
        [],
        [{stream, Filename}]
        ).
```

Using OAuth

Many websites now use OAuth to provide identity services. OAuth is a protocol that allows a user to authenticate from an external resource, such as Google or Facebook. To use OAuth, a program just needs to know the token from the server and httpc or another web client.

The way OAuth works is that your site redirects the user to a web page provided by the OAuth provider, and this site then prompts the user to approve your site's use of OAuth. Assuming the user authorizes the access, the user will be redirected back to your site with a token. If you then make an HTTP request to the providing site with that token, it will respond with a JSON that provides user information, including their name. See Example 8-4.

Example 8-4. Using OAuth (oauth.erl)

```
-module(oauth).

-export([auth/2]).


auth(Site, OAuthToken) ->
    URL = lists:flatten(io_lib:format("~s~s", [Site, OAuthToken])),
    io:format("~n~p:~p (~p)~n OAuth URL ~p~n", [?MODULE, ?LINE, self(), URL]),
    {ok, {{_Version, 200, _ReasonPhrase}, _Headers, Body}} = httpc:request(URL),
    {ok, JSON,_} = rfc4627:decode(Body),
    io:format("~n~p:~p (~p)~n JSON: ~p~n", [?MODULE, ?LINE, self(), JSON]),
    JSON.
```

In the case of the Facebook Canvas (see the next section), once the user has authorized, then when Facebook loads your Canvas page it will send a POST to the page with a JSON containing an OAuth token. (Full details are on Facebook's developer site.) Once you have that token, you can do an https request to the Facebook server, which will return a JSON like in Example 8-9. (Note that this JSON has been reformatted with JSON Lint and personal information has been removed.)

Facebook Canvas

If you are building a Facebook application, one way you can interact with Facebook is via the Canvas. When an application is opened by Facebook as a Canvas, it is opened in an iframe inside a page from Facebook. Inside that page your app can communicate with your server and do anything else you want it to do. You can also communicate with Facebook via their interfaces.

When Facebook opens a Canvas page, it sends you a POST containing a signed request that is a base64-encoded JSON allowing you to authenticate the user.

To use this data, get the signed_request field of the post data from Facebook and split it on the period. The first part is a signature that you use your secret key to validate, and the second part is the data to allow you to authenticate the user.

If the user has not authorized with your application, you will get a JSON like in Example 8-5. In this case you should redirect the user to the Facebook authentication dialog. (See Facebook's documentation for the details: *https://developers.facebook.com/docs/authentication/canvas/.*)

At this point you need to redirect the user to the Facebook authorization page.

Example 8-5. Initial JSON

```
{
    "algorithm": "HMAC-SHA256",
    "issued_at": 1335672795,
    "user": {
        "country": "il",
        "locale": "en_US",
        "age": {
            "min": 21
        }
    }
}
```

To implement this, use a page like Example 8-6, which generates a basic HTML page and then calls the code in Example 8-7 to unpack the request and send the JSON to any included JavaScript. (You probably also want to save the data in a session cookie.)

Example 8-6. Facebook interface Yaws file (facebook.yaws)

```
<!DOCTYPE html>
<html>
  <head>
    <meta    http-equiv    ="Content-Type"
         content    ="text/html; charset=UTF-8">
    <title>Canvas</title>
  </head>
  <body>
    <pre>
      <erl>
out(Arg) ->
    {ok, SignedRequest} = postvar(Arg, "signed_request"),
    ParsedRequest    = facebook:parse_signed_request(SignedRequest),
    facebook:response(facebook:user_has_authorized(ParsedRequest)).
      </erl>
    </pre>
  </body>
</html>
```

The code in Example 8-7 will implement the basics of a Facebook interface. It can decode the request from Facebook and interact with the OAuth servers.

Example 8-7. Facebook interface (facebook.erl)

```erlang
-module(facebook).


-export([parse_signed_request/1,
         user_has_authorized/1,
         make_redirect_script/0,
         get_user_id/1,
         get_user_info/1,
         response/1]).

-define(SECRET,         "*******************************").
-define(APP_ID,         "***************").
-define(APP_NAMESPACE,  "*************").


parse_signed_request(SignedRequest) ->
    [_EncodingSig, Payload]    = string:tokens(SignedRequest, "."),
    PayloadJson                = tt:fb_decode_base64(Payload),
    {ok, JSON, _}              = rfc4627:decode(PayloadJson),
    JSON.

user_has_authorized(ParsedRequest) ->
    rfc4627:get_field(ParsedRequest, "oauth_token", undefined).

get_user_id(ParsedRequest) ->
    rfc4627:get_field(ParsedRequest, "user_id", undefined).

make_user_redirect_url()->
    URLPatern      =
    "https://www.facebook.com/dialog/oauth/?client_id=~s&redirect_uri=~s&scope=~s",
    RedirectURL        = lists:flatten(io_lib:format( "https://apps.facebook.com/~s",
                            [?APP_NAMESPACE])),
    Permission_Names   = string:join(["user_interests",
                        "user_location",
                        "user_photos",
                        "user_hometown",
                        "email"],
                       ","),
    URL                 = io_lib:format(URLPatern,
                                   [?APP_ID,
                                    yaws_api:url_encode(RedirectURL),
                                    Permission_Names]),
    lists:flatten(URL).


make_redirect_script() ->
    Url       = make_user_redirect_url(),
    Tag       = "<a href=~p>~p</a>",
    Script    = io_lib:format(Tag, [Url,Url]),
    lists:flatten(Script).
```

```
get_user_info(OAuthToken) ->
    URL = lists:flatten("https://graph.facebook.com/me?access_token="
            ++ binary:bin_to_list(OAuthToken)),
    io:format("~n~p:~p (~p)~n OAuth URL ~p~n", [?MODULE, ?LINE, self(), URL]),
    {ok, {{_Version, 200, _ReasonPhrase}, _Headers, Body}} = httpc:request(URL),
    {ok, JSON,_} = rfc4627:decode(Body),
    io:format("~n~p:~p (~p)~n JSON: ~p~n", [?MODULE, ?LINE, self(), Body]),
    JSON.


response(undefined)->
    {html, facebook:make_redirect_script()};
response(OAuthToken) ->
    UserInfo    = get_user_info(OAuthToken),
    io:format("~n~p:~p (~p)~n JSON: ~p~n", [?MODULE, ?LINE, self(), UserInfo]),
    JSON        = rfc4627:encode(UserInfo),
    [
    {ehtml,  {script,[], "user_info_data = " ++ JSON}}].
```

Once the user has told Facebook that he wishes to allow your app to know who he is, Facebook will open your page with a JSON that looks like Example 8-8. Here you will note that there are two new fields. The first is the oauth_token that enables you to request the user's details from Facebook; the second is the user_id that can be used to track sessions and locally cache user information.

Example 8-8. Authorized JSON

```
{
    "algorithm": "HMAC-SHA256",
    "expires": 1335679200,
    "issued_at": 1335673105,
    "oauth_token": "AAAB9elehJ9...",
    "user": {
        "country": "il",
        "locale": "en_US",
        "age": {
            "min": 21
        }
    },
    "user_id": "100************"
}
```

See Example 8-9 for the data that Facebook sends back from an OAuth request if the user has allowed the app to authenticate. (Not that the JSON here has been reformatted to make it more readable.)

Example 8-9. Using OAuth (oauth.json)

```
{
    "id": "***************",
    "name": "Joshua Levi",
    "first_name": "Joshua",
    "last_name": "Levi",
```

```
    "link": "http:\\/\\/www.facebook.com\\/profile.php?id=***************",
    "gender": "male",
    "email": "zkessin\\u0040**********.***",
    "timezone": 3,
    "locale": "en_US",
    "updated_time": "2010-10-17T10:49:04+0000"
}
```

CHAPTER 9

Building an Application with OTP

So far this book has shown small pieces of Erlang or other code to demonstrate one idea or another. This chapter does something a bit different. Here I will develop a larger application to demonstrate how all the parts of an Erlang- and Yaws-based web application hang together.

This application will allow a bunch of users to notify each other of updates in status. Whenever a user's status changes in their browser or on their phone, that change will be made available by the server. It will also keep track of each user's status so when a user signs in, she can see all the existing status messages. This application can serve as the base of many distributed applications, and I hope it will prove illustrative of how to build an application in Erlang.

 Feel free to use this module as a basis for your own product. If you do something really cool with it, please let me know!

This application will also split the application into layers: we'll have a server level that will coordinate between the users, and a web frontend that will use a simple web interface.

In this chapter we'll build a more complex application using the standard Erlang/OTP structures. By doing this we can take advantage of the fact that OTP is a very well tested framework for building extremely robust servers, and match that with an interface in Yaws that can work with the web browser.

An OTP application features several parts, all of which must be present. First we have the *workers* that actually perform the tasks of the application—in this case, keeping track of user status messages.

But beyond our workers we also have some other processes. The first type is a *supervisor*. The supervisor exists to keep an eye on the workers—if a worker dies, the supervisor will restart the process, and the users will simply see a restarted server the next time they try to poll for a status.

To understand how this works, look at Figure 9-1. In this diagram each box represents a process and each process is responsible for those below it on the tree. Here the supervisors are depicted as squares while the workers are circles. If one of the processes were to die (which sooner or later will happen), its supervisor will restart it. The full setup does not have to be on one server, so it would be possible for the nodes on the right to be on one server while those on the left are on the other, thus giving us the ability to handle fallover. How to do that fully is beyond the scope of this book.

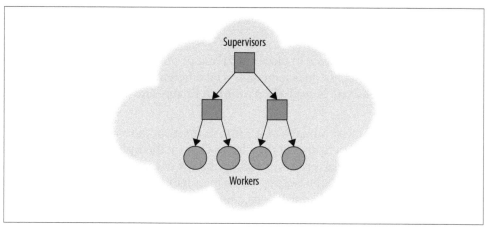

Figure 9-1. Supervision tree

Directory Structure

The OTP application wants files to be in a standard set of directories. These are *ebin*, *include*, *priv*, *src*, and *test*. Other directories can be added to this if needed.

The *ebin* directory is the only one that is actually required, and it should hold the *.beam* files as well as the *.app* file that describes the application (see "The App File" on page 115).

The *src* directory will hold all Erlang sources required for the applications. Any *.hrl* include files should be in the *include* directory. Testing code of course lives in the *test* directory.

The final directory is *priv*, which can contain any other resources that an application may need. This can include templates, config files, so forth. You can always get the application's *priv* directory by calling `code:priv_dir(Application)`.

Building an Application Server

When building an application in Erlang, I like to start by thinking about what kind of information is moving around the application. I will normally diagram this with pencil and paper or on a whiteboard. However, to save you the trouble of deciphering my handwriting I have translated it to a more readable form (see Figure 9-2).

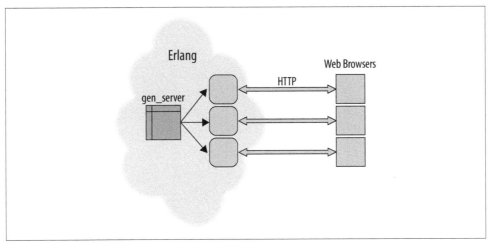

Figure 9-2. Data movement

This web application consists of a few parts, so let's look at it from the outside in. There is a part that runs in the web browser (covered in "Interfacing the Server with the Web" on page 101) that will communicate with the server via a web resource. The browsers are the right-hand squares on the right, the Yaws web servers are the rounded boxes in the middle, and the OTP server is the gen_server on the left of the diagram.

In this case we use a generic server as shown in "The Multicast Server" on page 96 to hold the state of each user. Users will update their status by periodically polling for changes over a web interface.

The Generic Server

The actual logic of an OTP application will consist of a collection of basic servers that will normally be written around the basic abstractions provided by the OTP library. The main one is gen_server, which is a generic server. The gen_server provides all the standard parts of a server, and all the developer has to do is create the functions that implement the features needed for the application in question.

Much like implementing an interface in Java, to implement gen_server a module must implement a few functions: start_link/0, init/1, handle_call/3, handle_cast/2, handle_info/2, terminate/2, code_change/3. If you use Emacs as your editor, Erlang mode will create this structure along with a number of others for you with a template. For an example of this template, take a look at Example D-3 in Appendix D. Many of the examples in this chapter are based on the Emacs templates.

To understand all of this, it helps to have a simple module to look at. Example 9-1 is a simple server that will generate sequential unique IDs.

Example 9-1. Generate unique IDS (uniq.erl)

```erlang
-module(uniq).
-behaviour(gen_server).

%% API
-export([start_link/0]).
-export([get_id/0]).
%% gen_server callbacks
-export([init/1,
     handle_call/3,
     handle_cast/2,
     handle_info/2,
     terminate/2,
     code_change/3]).

-define(SERVER, ?MODULE).

-record(state, {count}).

get_id() ->
    {id, ID} = gen_server:call(?MODULE, {}),
    ID.



%%%======================================================================
%%% API
%%%======================================================================

start_link() ->
    gen_server:start_link({local, ?SERVER}, ?MODULE, [], []).

init([]) ->
    {ok, #state{count= 1 }}.

handle_call(_Request, _From, State) ->
    Count = State#state.count,
    {reply,
     {id, Count},
     #state{count = Count + 1}}.

handle_cast(_Msg, State) ->
    {noreply, State}.

handle_info(_Info, State) ->
    {noreply, State}.

terminate(_Reason, _State) ->
```

```
        ok.

code_change(_OldVsn, State, _Extra) ->
    {ok, State}.
```

This server is started by calling start_link/0, which will initialize the server by calling the init/1 function. This always starts off the internal state of the server with count being 1.

This module exports one function API that consists of the function get_id/0. This function uses the gen_server:call/2 function to send a message requesting an ID from the server. Unlike using something like Pid ! get_id, this has an implicit timeout. If the server does not respond inside five seconds, gen_server:call/2 will die and leave a message. If this is not enough time (or too much), you can pass a third parameter that will let you specify a timeout. Pass the time in milliseconds or the atom infinity.

The handle_call function will be called when a message comes in that has to be responded to. In general this function will do something and return a tuple like {reply, Reply, NewState}.

> If you have programmed in Haskell or a similar language, you may notice that the gen_server looks a lot like a state monad.

All of the state that is used by the functions in the server is bound up in the State parameter that is passed in to the various functions; there are no other artifacts such as singletons in Java or the JavaScript window object. This may seem quite restrictive, but it actually enables some very powerful features.

> This also makes writing tests much easier! The handle_call function will normally be close to a pure function, with all the global state in one place both before and after. There is no chance for a strange side effect to go clobber something over there.

The OTP framework wraps messages that are sent in a structure that enables the gen_server to call both handle_cast and handle_call for different kinds of messages. However, if a message is sent to the server that is not wrapped by the gen_server framework it will be handled by handle_info/2.

If you do not need this functionality, then having a handle_info/2 function that will log any messages as errors will enable you to track down where they are being sent from. Or you could omit the handle_info/2 function altogether; you will get a warning when you compile but it can be ignored. In this case, when an unknown message is sent to the process gen_server will terminate the process and leave an error message. In general, this is what you want as the supervisor will recreate it (see "Let's Have Some Adult

Supervision Around Here!" on page 104). Remember, in Erlang, defensive programming is bad—we want a server that is going wrong to terminate so that the supervisor can start up a fresh copy with a known good state.

If your server needs to do any cleanup when it is done, use the `terminate/2` function. This can close database connections or flush buffers, remove temporary files, and so on. The first parameter of the `terminate/2` function will be the reason the process is being terminated—it could be because the supervisor was told to shut down, or is shutting down a number of workers, or a linked node is shutting down.[1]

The Multicast Server

In our application (Example 9-2) we have a fairly simple server implementation in `multi_cast_server`. This server keeps track of the most recent state of each user. As such, this function only has an external API of three functions: `get_current_user_sta tus/0`, which gets the status of all users on the system; `get_current_user_status/1`, which gets the status of a specific user; and `update_status/2`, which updates the user's status.

Each of these functions will send a message via the `gen_server:call/2` function to the server, which will reply with a clause of the `handle_call/3` function.

The `handle_call/3` function takes the three possible requests and the current state of the server and either updates the state or returns the requested information.

 This server has more logging in it than you might normally want. I like to put a lot of log statements in for development.

The actual state of the group is passed around as a `State` value to each element. In this case it is just an array, though in a more complex example it could be (and probably should be) a record for a more complex data structure. There are two functions that have been created to deal with this state: `update_user_status/3` and `get_user_status/2`.

Example 9-2. Multicast server

```
%%%-------------------------------------------------------------------
%%% @author Zach Kessin <>
%%% @copyright (C) 2012, Zach Kessin
%%% @doc
%%%
%%% @end
%%% Created : 21 Mar 2012 by Zach Kessin <>
```

---

1. See the manual page for the full details (*http://www.erlang.org/doc/man/gen_server.html#Module: terminate-2*).

```erlang
%%%-------------------------------------------------------------------
-module(multi_cast_server).

-behaviour(gen_server).

%% API
-export([start_link/0]).

-export([get_current_user_status/0,
    get_current_user_status/1,
    update_status/2]).

%% gen_server callbacks
-export([init/1, handle_call/3, handle_cast/2, handle_info/2,
    terminate/2, code_change/3]).

-define(SERVER, ?MODULE).




%%%===================================================================
%%% API
%%%--=================================================================

get_current_user_status() ->
    gen_server:call(?MODULE, {get_current_user_status}).


get_current_user_status(User) ->
    gen_server:call(?MODULE, {get_current_user_status, User}).


update_status(User, Status) ->
    ok = gen_server:call(?MODULE, {update_status, User, Status}),
    ok.

%%%===================================================================
%%% Functions for internal Use
%%%===================================================================

update_user_status([], User, Status) ->
    [{User, Status}];

update_user_status([{User, _OldStatus} | Tail], User, Status) ->
    [{User,Status} | Tail];

update_user_status([{O,S}|Tail], User, Status) ->
    R = update_user_status(Tail, User, Status),
    [{O,S}|R].

get_user_status(UserStatus, TargetUser) ->
    case lists:filter(fun({User,_Status}) ->
                    User == TargetUser
                end,
```

```
          UserStatus) of
    [] ->
        no_status;
    [TargetUserStatus] ->
        {ok, TargetUserStatus}
    end.


%%--------------------------------------------------------------------
%% @doc
%% Starts the server
%%
%% @spec start_link() -> {ok, Pid} | ignore | {error, Error}
%% @end
%%--------------------------------------------------------------------
start_link() ->
    gen_server:start_link({local, ?SERVER}, ?MODULE, [], []).


%%%===================================================================
%%% gen_server callbacks
%%%===================================================================


%%--------------------------------------------------------------------
%% @private
%% @doc
%% Initializes the server
%%
%% @spec init(Args) -> {ok, State} |
%%                     {ok, State, Timeout} |
%%                     ignore |
%%                     {stop, Reason}
%% @end
%%--------------------------------------------------------------------


init([]) ->
    io:format("~n~p:~p(~p) init(~p)~n",
        [?MODULE, ?LINE, self(), []]),

    {ok, []};

init(Status) ->
    io:format("~n~p:~p(~p) init(~p)~n",
        [?MODULE, ?LINE, self(), Status]),
    {ok, Status}.

%%--------------------------------------------------------------------
%% @private
%% @doc
%% Handling call messages
%%
%% @spec handle_call(Request, From, State) ->
%%                                  {reply, Reply, State} |
%%                                  {reply, Reply, State, Timeout} |
%%                                  {noreply, State} |
```

```erlang
%%                                      {noreply, State, Timeout} |
%%                                      {stop, Reason, Reply, State} |
%%                                      {stop, Reason, State}
%% @end
%%--------------------------------------------------------------------


handle_call({get_current_user_status}, _From, State) ->
    {reply,
     {ok, State},
     State};

handle_call({get_current_user_status, User}, _From, State) ->
    {reply,
     get_user_status(State, User),
     State};


handle_call({update_status, User, Status}, _From, State) ->
    io:format("~p:~p (~p) Update ~p -> ~p ~n",
          [?MODULE, ?LINE, self(), User, Status]),
    io:format("STATE ~p ~n", [State]),
    NewState = update_user_status(State, User, Status),
    {reply, ok, NewState}.

%%--------------------------------------------------------------------
%% @private
%% @doc
%% Handling cast messages
%%
%% @spec handle_cast(Msg, State) -> {noreply, State} |
%%                                  {noreply, State, Timeout} |
%%                                  {stop, Reason, State}
%% @end
%%--------------------------------------------------------------------
handle_cast(_Msg, State) ->
    {noreply, State}.

%%--------------------------------------------------------------------
%% @private
%% @doc
%% Handling all non call/cast messages
%%
%% @spec handle_info(Info, State) -> {noreply, State} |
%%                                   {noreply, State, Timeout} |
%%                                   {stop, Reason, State}
%% @end
%%--------------------------------------------------------------------
handle_info(_Info, State) ->
    {noreply, State}.

%%--------------------------------------------------------------------
%% @private
%% @doc
%% This function is called by a gen_server when it is about to
```

```
%% terminate. It should be the opposite of Module:init/1 and do any
%% necessary cleaning up. When it returns, the gen_server terminates
%% with Reason. The return value is ignored.
%%
%% @spec terminate(Reason, State) -> void()
%% @end
%%--------------------------------------------------------------------
terminate(_Reason, _State) ->
    ok.


%%--------------------------------------------------------------------
%% @private
%% @doc
%% Convert process state when code is changed
%%
%% @spec code_change(OldVsn, State, Extra) -> {ok, NewState}
%% @end
%%--------------------------------------------------------------------
code_change(_OldVsn, State, _Extra) ->
    {ok, State}.


%%%===================================================================
%%% Internal functions
%%%===================================================================
```

When developing this module I first exposed those two functions with an `-export()`
directive and made sure that they did the right thing on test data by trying out a number
of test cases. Once I was sure that these two functions worked as they should, I removed
the export module and started up the server. I then tried a number of examples from
the Erlang command line, as summarized in Example 9-3. In fact I literally cut and
pasted this code from an Emacs buffer into Yaws, which was running in an Emacs shell
buffer. It crashed my server with an error, I fixed that bug, and repeated until everything
worked.

Example 9-3. Multicast server test

```
c(multi_cast_server).
multi_cast_server:start_link().
multi_cast_server:update_status("Zach","Testing").
multi_cast_server:update_status("Nati","TV").
multi_cast_server:update_status("Zach","Coding").
multi_cast_server:get_current_user_status("Zach").
multi_cast_server:get_current_user_status().
```

 In addition to the generic server (gen_server), there is also a generic finite
state machine (gen_fsm) implementation and a lot more in the OTP
framework. These are beyond the scope of this book, but *Learn You
Some Erlang* and the Erlang documentation cover them quite well.

Interfacing the Server with the Web

So far we have a bunch of Erlang services that are kind of interesting but not particularly useful in and of themselves, as they can't interface with the outside world—which is, after all, what we want to do. So we need to write some code to provide a web interface onto all of this.

To do this we will first add an *htdocs* directory to the standard set of Yaws directories. This directory can contain all the public facing files of the web service including *.yaws* files, images, CSS, JavaScript, and so forth.

 In this case we will connect the *htdocs* dir to the Yaws document root via a symlink, but we could also do it in the *yaws.conf* file. It is also possible to run Yaws as an OTP app inside an existing Erlang setup, but this is beyond the scope of this book.

The first file, shown in Example 9-4, is a simple one that calls the `multi_cast_server:get_current_user_status/0` function and then formats the result as a JSON for the server with the function `convert_to_json/1`. Note that the strings are converted to binaries with the `list_to_binary/1` function that is built into Erlang. If you don't do this then you will get back an array of integers in the JSON, which is probably not what you had in mind.

Example 9-4. Get status (status.yaws)

```
<erl>
convert_to_json(Data) ->
    Content = [{obj, [{name,   list_to_binary(Name)},
            {status, list_to_binary(Status)}]} ||
        {Name, Status} <-Data],
    {obj, [{data, Content}]}.


out(_Arg) ->
    {ok, Obj} = multi_cast_server:get_current_user_status(),
    io:format("~n (~p) Raw Data ~p~n", [self(), Obj]),
    JSON = rfc4627:encode(convert_to_json(Obj)),
    io:format("~n (~p) JSON ->  ~p~n", [self(), JSON]),
    {content, "application/json", JSON}.
</erl>
```

Once again we have some extra log information in this example; the output from the logs can be found in Example 9-5. Here you can see the raw data that comes back from the server, and the JSON into which it has been converted (extra whitespace has been added).

Example 9-5. Get status log data

```
(<0.365.0>) Raw Data [{"Zach","Coding"},{"Nati","TV"}]
(<0.365.0>) JSON ->
    "[{\"name\":\"Zach\",\"status\":\"Coding\"},{\"name\":\"Nati\",\"status\":\"TV\"}]"
```

The users can get the status of other users by sending a GET to Example 9-4. This is a very simple *.yaws* file that serves only to call the server and then translate the returned data into the JSON that the client will expect.

To set the status of a user, the browser will send a POST request to "set-status.yaws" (Example 9-6). As above, this file contains only enough code to decode the user's request and pass the data on to the server.

Example 9-6. Set status (set-status.yaws)

```
<erl>
out(Arg) ->
    {ok, Name}   = postvar(Arg, "name"),
    {ok, Status} = postvar(Arg, "status"),
    io:format("~n(~p) Name ~p, Status ~p ~n",
        [self(), Name, Status]),
    multi_cast_server:update_status(Name, Status),
    {html, "true"}.


</erl>
```

Some Client-Side Code

For the client-side code we are going to keep it very simple. Using ExtJS we will construct a simple interface that will show the current status of all the users in a grid. At the bottom of the grid will be a field where users can enter their current status.

In Figure 9-3, the browser application displays the current status of the various users with an interface written in ExtJS. The CoffeeScript code in Example 9-7 shows a basic interface of a grid displaying each user along with their status.

The interface also has a form allowing the user to set his or her status. This example lets you set the status for any user; a more robust example should of course use some authentication to determine the user.

Example 9-7. Socket handler (socket_handler.coffee)

```
makeStore = ->
        store = Ext.create("Ext.data.Store",
                autoLoad : true
                fields   : ["name","status"]
                proxy    :
                        type   : "ajax"
                        url    : "status.yaws"
                        reader :
```

```
                                       type: "json"
                                       root: "data"
                       )
           console.log(store)
           store

setupMultiCast = ->
           store = makeStore()
           form  - Ext.create("Ext.form.Panel",
                   buttons:
                           {
                                       xtype: "button"
                                       text: "Set Status"
                                       handler: () ->
                                               values = form.getValues()
                                               console.log(values)
                                               Ext.Ajax.request(
                                                       url: "set-status.yaws",
                                                       params: values
                                                       success: () ->
                                                               store.load()
                                                               alert("Data Reloaded")
                                               )


                           }
                   title: "Set Status"
                   items: [
                           {
                                       xtype      : "textfield"
                                       name       : "name"
                                       fieldLabel : "User"
                                       width      : 400
                           }
                           {
                                       xtype      : "textarea"
                                       name       : "status"
                                       fieldLabel : "Status"
                                       width      : 400

                           }
                           ]
           )

           grid  = Ext.create("Ext.grid.Panel",
                   width     : 500
                   height    : 350,
                   frame     : true
                   renderTo  : "multi_cast"
                   store     : store
                   title     : "User Status"
                   bbar      : form
                   buttons   : [
                           {
                                       text: "Reload"
                                       handler: () -> store.load()
```

```
                }]

        columns:
                [
                        {
                                text: "User"
                                width: 80
                                sortable: true
                                dataIndex: "name"
                        }
                        {
                                text: "Status"
                                dataIndex: "status"
                                sortable: true
                                width: 300
                        }
                ]

        )

Ext.onReady setupMultiCast
```

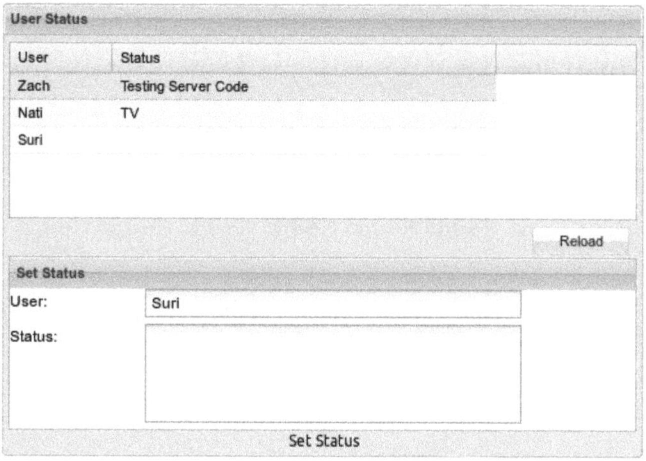

Figure 9-3. Multicast application

Let's Have Some Adult Supervision Around Here!

Our server will run for a long time distributing messages between various users. Sooner or later something will go wrong. If that happens the process will terminate, and we want to define what happens next. In this case, several things need to happen: first of all, the server should be restarted, and we also want to log what happened so we can fix it later.

OTP uses the concept of a supervisor to do all of these things, and thankfully building a basic supervisor is pretty easy. The basic supervisor is the **supervisor** behavior. Like a gen_server, you just need to create a module that exports a few functions, and also like a gen_server, the Emacs Erlang mode will create a template you can use. Example 9-8 is based on the Emacs template with some of the comments removed for space.

Example 9-8. Setting up our Supervisor

```
%%%-------------------------------------------------------------------
%%% @author Zach Kessin <>
%%% @copyright (C) 2012, Zach Kessin
%%% @doc
%%%
%%% @end
%%% Created : 18 Mar 2012 by Zach Kessin <>
%%%-------------------------------------------------------------------
-module(multi_cast_sup).

-behaviour(supervisor).

%% API
-export([start_link/0]).

%% Supervisor callbacks
-export([init/1]).

-define(SERVER, ?MODULE).

%%%===================================================================
%%% API functions
%%%===================================================================

%%--------------------------------------------------------------------
%% @doc
%% Starts the supervisor
%%--------------------------------------------------------------------
start_link() ->
    supervisor:start_link({local, ?SERVER}, ?MODULE, []).

%%%===================================================================
%%% Supervisor callbacks
%%%===================================================================

%%--------------------------------------------------------------------
%% @private
%% @doc
%% Whenever a supervisor is started using supervisor:start_link/[2,3],
%% this function is called by the new process to find out about
%% restart strategy, maximum restart frequency and child
%% specifications.
%%
%% @spec init(Args) -> {ok, {SupFlags, [ChildSpec]}} |
%%                     ignore |
%%                     {error, Reason}
```

```
%% @end
%%--------------------------------------------------------------------
init([]) ->
    RestartStrategy              = one_for_one,
    MaxRestarts                  = 1000,
    MaxSecondsBetweenRestarts    = 3600,

    SupFlags                     = {RestartStrategy,
                                     MaxRestarts,
                                     MaxSecondsBetweenRestarts},

    Restart                      = permanent,
    Shutdown                     = 2000,
    Type                         = worker,

    AChild                       = {'process_id',
                                     {'AModule', start_link, []},
                                     Restart,
                                     Shutdown,
                                     Type,
                                     ['AModule']},

    {ok, {SupFlags, [AChild]}}.


%%%===================================================================
%%% Internal functions
%%%===================================================================
```

When creating a supervisor, you need to create a module that exports an init/1 function. This function is called when the supervisor starts up and defines the rules for how and when workers are created and restarted.

The supervisor is run as its own process that does nothing but monitor other processes (these can be other supervisors or the ones doing the actual work). When these other processes die, the supervisor will restart them; it can also kill them when it's time to shut down an application.

In addition, the supervisor is where worker processes are started. This is done by listing the processes in the supervisor init/1 function as part of the return value. For each process we get a structure like in Example 9-9. The first field is a process ID that is used by the supervisor internally; it may show up in listings but you can probably ignore it. The second term tells how to start our server. It should contain the module, the function to start the module (normally start_link), and any parameters to pass to that function.

Example 9-9. Process init structure

```
{
  Process_id,
  {Module, start_link, []},
  Restart,
  Shutdown,
  Type,
```

```
[Module]
}
```

The Restart term tells the supervisor how and when to restart this server if needed. Options are permanent, temporary, and transient. A permanent process will always be restarted. A temporary process will never be restarted. A transient process will be restarted if it dies unexpectedly, but if it terminates normally it will not be restarted.

The supervisor includes protection against a process that is stuck restarting itself and instantly exiting. If you set the MaxR and MaxT values it will limit the process to a set number of restarts in a period of time. In our example we limit the number of restarts to 1000 per hour; in a production system these numbers will need to be adjusted for the specifics of the application.

The Shutdown term comes into play when it is time to shut down an application. When an application is being shut down worker, processes may need to close resources or otherwise clean up. As such, the supervisor should allow time to do that. In this case, set Shutdown to a time in milliseconds for how long each process can take before the supervisor will kill it outright. To kill a process with no warning set this to bru tal_kill; if the processes may need a very long time, set this to infinity. Getting this setting right may take some fine-tuning.

The Type parameter can have two possible values: worker or supervisor. That is, the process can be a worker or a lower level of supervision.

Finally we have a list of modules. Normally this will be the same module as used above unless we are doing something weird and dynamic, in which case it might be the atom dynamic.

Now that we have our supervisor built we need to test it out. To do this we want to make our server die due to a bug and see that it restarted. So we'll introduce a new clause in the update_user_status/3 function that will cause the process to crash when a user sets a blank status message:

```
update_user_status(_users,_User, "") ->
    ok = status;
```

As you can see in Example 9-10, when we set the user's status to an empty string, we get an error and the process terminates.

 When running this from the Erlang shell, run unlink(SupervisorPid). before testing restarts. Otherwise the crashing process will also crash the shell (which restarts) and the supervisor.

Example 9-10. Running the supervisor

```
2> multi_cast_server:start_link().
{ok,<0.63.0>}
3> multi_cast_server:update_status("Zach","").
multi_cast_server:136 (<0.63.0>) Update "Zach" -> []
```

```
STATE []

=ERROR REPORT==== 3-Apr-2012::13:04:00 ===
** Generic server multi_cast_server terminating
** Last message in was {update_status,"Zach",[]}
** When Server state == []
** Reason for termination ==
** {{badmatch,status},
   [{multi_cast_server,update_user_status,3},
    {multi_cast_server,handle_call,3},
    {gen_server,handle_msg,5},
    {proc_lib,init_p_do_apply,3}]}
** exception exit: {badmatch,status}
    in function  multi_cast_server:update_user_status/3
    in call from multi_cast_server:handle_call/3
    in call from gen_server:handle_msg/5
    in call from proc_lib:init_p_do_apply/3
```

Ideally, you want each unit of work that can crash to be in its own process so that the smallest possible unit of work will crash. In this case we could take the function to create the updated state and put it in its own stateless process that would simply take a state, update it, and return it.

A Little Optimization

If you want to enhance this module for more speed, create a second module that will cache the JSON and create a hash of the data as an ETag. Then have the browser send a request with an HTTP IF-None-Match header, and if the data has not changed it will just get back an HTTP 304 header and use the data that it already has. And the nice thing is that the server will not have to compute the hash or create the JSON for each request, but can do it only when data is changed.

For Etags to be effective they need to be consistent. If each time the user makes a request she is shown a different server that has a different value, then the Etag will be useless. So in order for this to work, the load balancer needs to make sure that the same user is always shown the same server, or that there is some other mechanism for making sure that the user sees consistent data from the ETag.

This server keeps track of two pieces of information: the output JSON, and an MD5 hash that will be used by the browser to determine if it has up-to-date data.

The crypto:md5/1 function returns an array of numbers that is the raw hash of the data. We use the base64:encode_to_string/1 function to turn it into a string like "4CNCRcsAqiYMz6mamgsjXg==", which looks like something one would expect to get from MD5.

We also get an additional bit of reliability here. We can set this up so that when this server crashes it will just restart and have the init/1 function automatically query the server that holds the data to refresh it. On the other hand, if that server crashes we can set it so that this server will also be restarted so there is no stale data. This is done in Example 9-11, which creates a server to create the JSON data.

Example 9-11. Caching the results (multi_cast_front)

```erlang
%%%-------------------------------------------------------------------
%%% @author Zach Kessin <>
%%% @copyright (C) 2012, Zach Kessin
%%% @doc
%%%
%%% @end
%%% Created :  5 Apr 2012 by Zach Kessin <>
%%%-------------------------------------------------------------------
-module(multi_cast_front).

-behaviour(gen_server).

%% API
-export([start_link/0]).

%% gen_server callbacks
-export([init/1, handle_call/3, handle_cast/2, handle_info/2,
        terminate/2, code_change/3]).
-export([get_json/0, get_etag/0, update_status/2]).
-export([convert_to_json/1, make_state/0]).
-define(SERVER, ?MODULE).



-record(state, {etag, json}).

get_json() ->
    gen_server:call(?MODULE, {get_json}).

get_etag() ->
    gen_server:call(?MODULE, {get_etag}).

update_status(User, Status) ->
    multi_cast_server:update_status(User, Status),
    gen_server:call(?MODULE, {update_status}).


%%%===================================================================
%%% API
%%%===================================================================

%%--------------------------------------------------------------------
%% @doc
%% Starts the server
%%
%% @spec start_link() -> {ok, Pid} | ignore | {error, Error}
```

```erlang
%% @end
%%------------------------------------------------------------------
start_link() ->
    gen_server:start_link({local, ?SERVER}, ?MODULE, [], []).


%%%==================================================================
%%% gen_server callbacks
%%%==================================================================


init([]) ->
    io:format("~n~p:~p(~p) init(~p)~n",
            [?MODULE, ?LINE, self(), []]),

    State = make_state(),
    {ok, State}.

handle_call({get_json}, _From, State) ->
    {reply, State#state.json, State};

handle_call({get_etag}, _From, State) ->
    {reply, State#state.etag, State};

handle_call({update_status}, _From, _State) ->
    NewState = make_state(),
    {noreply, NewState}.



handle_cast(_Msg, State) ->
    {noreply, State}.

handle_info(_Info, State) ->
    {noreply, State}.

terminate(_Reason, _State) ->
    ok.

code_change(_OldVsn, State, _Extra) ->
    {ok, State}.

%%%==================================================================
%%% Internal functions
%%%==================================================================

convert_to_json(Data) ->
    Content = [{obj, [
                {name,   list_to_binary(Name)},
                {status, list_to_binary(Status)}]} ||
            {Name, Status} <-Data],
    {obj, [{data, Content}]}.


make_state () ->
    {ok, Data}    = multi_cast_server:get_current_user_status(),
```

```
    io:format("~n~p:~p(~p) new data   ~p~n",
        [?MODULE, ?LINE, self(), Data]),

    Json    = rfc4627:encode(convert_to_json(Data)),
    Etag    = base64:encode_to_string(crypto:md5(Json)),
    io:format("~n~p:~p(~p) new data Etag: ~p ~p~n",
        [?MODULE, ?LINE, self(), Etag, Json]),
    NewState    = #state{
      json = Json,
      etag = Etag},
    NewState.
```

We also need to change the supervisor in Example 9-8 so that it will start both servers and restart them in the correct way. I have added a second server under the name "Front" in addition to the initial server we had in the first example.

I have also changed the restart strategy from one_for_one to rest_for_one. This ensures that since the frontend server is started after the main server it will be restarted if the main one is, but not the other way around. This new supervisor is shown in Example 9-12.

Example 9-12. Setting up our supervisor (Take 2)

```
-module(multi_cast_sup2).

-behaviour(supervisor).

%% API
-export([start_link/0]).

%% Supervisor callbacks
-export([init/1]).

-define(SERVER, ?MODULE).

%%%===================================================================
%%% API functions
%%%===================================================================


%%--------------------------------------------------------------------
%% @doc
%% Starts the supervisor
%%--------------------------------------------------------------------
start_link() ->
    supervisor:start_link({local, ?SERVER}, ?MODULE, []).

%%%===================================================================
%%% Supervisor callbacks
%%%===================================================================

init([]) ->
    io:format("~n~p:~p (~p) init([]) ~n",
        [?MODULE, ?LINE, self()]),
```

```
RestartStrategy                   = rest_for_one,
MaxRestarts                       = 1000,
MaxSecondsBetweenRestarts   = 3600,
ServerName              = multi_cast_server,
ServerFrontName                 = multi_cast_front,
SupFlags                          = {RestartStrategy,
                                        MaxRestarts,
                                        MaxSecondsBetweenRestarts},

Restart                           = permanent,
Shutdown                          = 2000,
Type                              = worker,

Server                            = {'multi_cast_server_id',
                                        {ServerName, start_link, []},
                                        Restart,
                                        Shutdown,
                                        Type,
                                        [ServerName]},
Front                           ={'multi_cast_front_id',
                                        {ServerFrontName, start_link, []},
                                        Restart,
                                        Shutdown,
                                        Type,
                                        [ServerFrontName]},
{ok, {SupFlags, [Server, Front]}}.


%%%=====================================================================
%%% Internal functions
%%%=====================================================================
```

We will also need to change the status.yaws and set-status.yaws files (Examples 9-4 and 9-6)to reflect the new interfaces.

The case of set-status.yaws is pretty simple, as we just need to change the call from multi_cast_server:update_status/2 to multi_cast_front:update_status/2 (see Example 9-13).

Example 9-13. Setting the status with the front controller (set-status2.yaws)

```
<erl>
out(Arg) ->
    {ok, Name}   = postvar(Arg, "name"),
    {ok, Status} = postvar(Arg, "status"),
    io:format("~n(~p) Name ~p, Status ~p ~n",
        [self(), Name, Status]),
    multi_cast_front:update_status(Name, Status),
    {html, "true"}.


</erl>
```

However, we have a bit of extra work to do in `status2.yaws`. Here we no longer have to convert the data to JSON ourselves, but we do have to check for a cache hit. If the browser sends an `If-None-Match` header, we will get the value of that header and compare it to the ETag that has been stored on the server. If they are the same, we should send back the 304 status code and tell the browser to use its cached copy of the data; otherwise we send back the actual data, and of course set an ETag in the header.

Example 9-14. Getting status with ETags (status2.yaws)

```erlang
<erl>

get_etag_header(Arg) ->
    Headers = Arg#arg.headers,
    Headers#headers.if_none_match.

get_response(Current_Etag, Header_Etag)
  when Current_Etag =:= Header_Etag ->
    {status, 304};
get_response(Current_Etag, _Header_Etag) ->
    JSON = multi_cast_front:get_json(),
    io:format("~n (~p) JSON ->  ~p~n", [self(), JSON]),
    [
     {content, "application/json", JSON},
     {header, "Etag: "++ Current_Etag}
    ].

out(Arg) ->
    Header_Etag     = get_etag_header(Arg),
    Current_Etag    = multi_cast_front:get_etag(),
    io:format("~n (~p) If-None-Match: ~p ~n", [self(), Header_Etag]),
    io:format("~n (~p) ETag:  ~p ~n", [self(), Current_Etag]),
    get_response(Current_Etag, Header_Etag).
</erl>
```

When the code in Example 9-14 is run, the response will look like Example 9-15 if the `If-None-Match` header is not set or if it does not match.

Example 9-15. The output from Example 9-14

```
HTTP/1.1 200 OK
Server: Yaws/1.92 Yet Another Web Server
Date: Tue, 10 Apr 2012 15:44:58 GMT
Content-Length: 12
Content-Type: application/json
Etag: 4CNCRcsAqiYMz6mamgsjXg==

{"data":[]}
```

If the header does match then the system will return Example 9-16, which will let the client know that the data has not changed.

Example 9-16. Cache hit from Example 9-14

```
HTTP/1.1 304 Not Modified
Server: Yaws/1.92 Yet Another Web Server
Date: Tue, 10 Apr 2012 15:49:30 GMT
Content-Length: 1
Content-Type: text/html
```

Bundling as an Application

When we take the supervisors ("Let's Have Some Adult Supervision Around Here!" on page 104) and the actual workers, we can package them together into an "application" that can be started and stopped in a standard way by Erlang. Once you do this, your application servers can be started by calling `application:start/1,2`. Pass it the name of the application to start and, if needed, an array containing any parameters that should be passed when starting the application.

The application behavior can be in the same module as the supervisor, as they share no function names, but it is probably better to leave them separate. In general the application should be named `APPNAME_app.erl` and the supervisor `APPNAME_sup.erl`.

 Erlang uses the term "application" to refer to a related set of services. Not to be confused with the more conventional use of the term.

To create an application, we use the application template from Emacs. The application behavior has two functions called `start/2` and `stop/1`. The start function will be called when the application is started, and the stop function is called when the application is stopped. Normally these will be used for setup and cleanup.

Example 9-17. Setting up our application

```
%%%-------------------------------------------------------------------
%%% @author Zach Kessin <>
%%% @copyright (C) 2012, Zach Kessin
%%% @doc
%%%
%%% @end
%%% Created : 18 Mar 2012 by Zach Kessin <>
%%%-------------------------------------------------------------------
-module(multi_cast_app).

-behaviour(application).

%% Application callbacks
-export([start/2, stop/1]).

%%%===================================================================
%%% Application callbacks
```

```
%%%=====================================================================

%%---------------------------------------------------------------------
%% @private
%% @doc
%% This function is called whenever an application is started using
%% application:start/[1,2], and should start the processes of the
%% application. If the application is structured according to the OTP
%% design principles as a supervision tree, this means starting the
%% top supervisor of the tree.
%%
%% @spec start(StartType, StartArgs) -> {ok, Pid} |
%%                                      {ok, Pid, State} |
%%                                      {error, Reason}
%%      StartType = normal | {takeover, Node} | {failover, Node}
%%      StartArgs = term()
%% @end
%%---------------------------------------------------------------------
start(_StartType, _StartArgs) ->
    io:format("~n~p:~p (~p) start(~p, ~p) ~n",
              [?MODULE, ?LINE, self(), _StartType, _StartArgs]),
    case multi_cast_sup2:start_link() of
        {ok, Pid} ->
            {ok, Pid};
        Error ->
            Error
                end.

%%---------------------------------------------------------------------
%% @private
%% @doc
%% This function is called whenever an application has stopped. It
%% is intended to be the opposite of Module:start/2 and should do
%% any necessary cleaning up. The return value is ignored.
%%
%% @spec stop(State) -> void()
%% @end
%%---------------------------------------------------------------------
stop(_State) ->
    ok.

%%%=====================================================================
%%% Internal functions
%%%=====================================================================
```

The App File

Every application in Erlang has an application file that lives in the *ebin* directory. This file will consist of a big data structure that looks like Example 9-18. The file should normally be titled something like my_app_name.app—in our case multi_cast.app.

This file has a number of fields, and in practice when creating one you will want to pull up the documentation as to what each field means, or base a new file on an older example.

The tuple starts with the atom `application`, followed by an atom that is the name of the application. After that is a large property list with a few key fields. The `description` field is a description of the application. The `vsn` field is the version number of the application. The next field, `modules`, will contain a list of the modules that an application uses. OTP will ensure that a module belongs to only one application and that all of these modules are present. Some of these applications will be server processes and others can be just groups of functions. Listing those modules here will ensure that the system will let you know if they are absent.

The `registered` field contains a list of the names registered by an application. This is useful because if two applications try to register the same name, OTP will know that and issue a warning.

The final item is `mod`, which is the callback module with the `application` behavior. If your app does not have any services that need to be started (for example if it's just a bunch of pure functions), omit this line.

 The Example 9-18 file must have a period (".") at the end or it won't work, and will give a really cryptic-looking error message.

Example 9-18. Setting up our application (multi_cast.app)

```
{
  application,
  multi_cast,
  [
   {description, "Multi Cast Example"},
   {vsn, "1.0.0"},
   {modules,
    [
     multi_cast_app,
     multi_cast_sup2,
     multi_cast_server,
     multi_cast_front
    ]},
   {registered, [multi_cast_server, multi_cast_front, multi_cast_sup2]},
   {mod, {multi_cast_app, []}}
  ]
}.
```

Once our applications have been defined and tested from the command line, we can set up Erlang to automatically start our application when it starts. This can be done by adding the like `application:start(MyApplication).` to the *.erlang* file or by passing a flag to the Erlang VM on starting.

The application framework also provides us a clean way to start, stop, and upgrade our application with all its dependencies.

Wrapping Up OTP

This chapter is not a full introduction to OTP, nor was it intended to be. However, I wanted to introduce some of the basic structure of OTP as a way to show how to structure an application.

The application we built in this chapter has some inherent limits; for one thing, the user's status is stored in a list, which makes updates an $O(N)$ operation. Since I intended to use this where the number of items in the list is small, fewer than 25 or so, it should not be a major problem. It would of course be possible to change the data structure to use a different data structure if needed.

In addition, this application assumes that only one copy of the servers will be running on a node. A more realistic goal would be to have a master supervisor that would create a supervisor and servers for each group of users. In such a case we would have a large number of groups of users, each with their own servers and supervisor. Above those would be one master supervisor that would restart the local supervisor if needed, which could then restart the servers.

In short, there are many things that were not covered here. I did not cover gen_fsm or gen_event, but these can provide other types of servers to nicely complement the gen_server.

Installing Erlang and Yaws

Erlang can be installed from *http://www.erlang.org*. There are versions for Mac, Linux, and Windows. In addition, most popular Linux distributions have packages for Erlang. As of this writing, the current version is R15B01.

Many modern Linux distributions will feature Erlang and Yaws in their basic package system. So from Ubuntu, doing a simple `sudo apt-get install yaws` will install Erlang and Yaws (and any dependencies). Similarly, Fedora Linux includes both Erlang and Yaws as part of the basic packages, which can be installed via `yum`.

Yaws can be found at *http://yaws.hyber.org* and downloaded from there. Once again, most Linux distributions will include packages. As of January 2012, the current version is 1.92.

In Ubuntu Linux, doing a simple `apt-get install yaws` will install Yaws with all the dependencies, including Erlang itself.

For Microsoft Windows, there are installers for Yaws that can be downloaded from *http://yaws.hyber.org*. However, before Yaws can run, Erlang itself must be downloaded separately.

Beyond Yaws

This book has been an introduction to using Yaws with Erlang. However, there are a number of other web servers and frameworks for Erlang that may make more sense for a specific project.

Web Servers

In addition to Yaws, there are two other Erlang web servers in active development: Cowboy and MochiWeb. Each has a different set of pros and cons that should be considered.

A detailed comparison of different Erlang web server options could be a book in and of itself. However, a good place to start is *http://www.ostinelli.net/a-comparison-be tween-misultin-mochiweb-cowboy-nodejs-and-tornadoweb/*, which attempts to compare Misultin, MochiWeb, and Cowboy along with Node.js (JavaScript) and Tornadoweb (Python).

Cowboy

Cowboy (*https://github.com/extend/cowboy*) is a new web server for Erlang designed to be small, fast, and modular. It is also designed to be easy to embed in other applications, which can be useful if you are creating a web interface to a larger Erlang application.

To set up a Cowboy server you must create some socket listeners and handlers to deal with incoming requests. So compared to Yaws, there is a bit more upfront set up required, you can't just give it a bunch of static files or embed Erlang in *.yaws* files and go. You must explicitly tell it how to handle requests.

Cowboy can also handle web sockets, and there is example code on the Cowboy GitHub page; however, work is still ongoing on that project. It is unclear how much support there is for file uploads, streaming data, and the like.

MochiWeb

MochiWeb (*https://github.com/mochi/mochiweb*) is not so much a web server as a set of components for building web servers. As such, it does not include many things that are included with Yaws, such as a URL dispatcher; you will have to create that on your own.

That being said, MochiWeb has a dedicated following on the Web, and many of the web frameworks use it as a base. You can find a MochiWeb tutorial at *https://github .com/mochi/mochiweb*.

Misultin

Misultin is an Erlang web server that has unfortunately been discontinued. The developers felt that with Cowboy, MochiWeb, and others running around that supporting yet another Erlang web server was too much duplicated effort. As such, they are supporting existing users but suggesting that everyone move to Cowboy ("Cowboy" on page 121) or MochiWeb ("MochiWeb" on page 122). Several of the frameworks for Erlang can run on Misultin, but most can also run on MochiWeb or Yaws.

Web Frameworks

There are currently at least six Erlang web frameworks that can be used: BeepBeep, Chicago Boss, Erlang Web, ErlyWeb, Nitrogen, and Zotonic. The Chicago Boss team maintains a high-level grid showing what frameworks support which features that can be found here: *https://github.com/evanmiller/ChicagoBoss/wiki/Comparison-of-Erlang -Web-Frameworks*.

BeepBeep, Erlang Web, and ErlyWeb seem to have not been updated since 2008 or 2009, so I am not going to cover them further.

Chicago Boss

Chicago Boss (*http://www.chicagoboss.org*) is a full-featured web framework originally built around Misultin and currently moving to Cowboy. It is under active development, has a nice website with a great tutorial, and has a lot of flexibility.

Chicago Boss is built around an MVC architecture, which should feel familiar to programmers who have used other MVC frameworks like Symfony on PHP or Ruby on Rails. It also features a built-in Queue system called "BossMQ" that can be used to link pieces of a larger application. Using BossMQ is as simple as calling `boss_mq:push/2` to add a message to a queue and `boss_mq:pull/2` to get a message from the queue. (For more details, see the Chicago Boss website.) This can be used with long polling, but for now it does not appear that Chicago Boss supports web sockets.

In terms of data storage, Chicago Boss features a lot of options. You can store your data in Mnesia, MongoDB, MySQL, PostgreSQL, Riak, or Tokyo Tyrant. It also uses ErlyDTL ("ErlyDTL" on page 26) for templates.

In general, Chicago Boss seems to be very well thought out and has a solid website with well-written documentation.

Nitrogen

Nitrogen (*http://nitrogenproject.com/*) is an event-based framework created by Rusty Klophaus. It uses its own template system instead of ErlyDTL or the like. It also seems to want to generate HTML in Erlang, while many modern systems will want to send JSON data to the browser and have the "View" layer running in a browser.

Zotonic

Zotonic (*http://zotonic.com*) is a CMS and framework for Erlang, and if you have used Drupal, it will probably feel pretty familiar. It features a rich set of management screens to allow a nondeveloper to manage a Zotonic website. It advertises a lot of features out of the box and is under active development. If you want to present web content with an Erlang backend, Zotonic may be a great choice!

Zotonic is built on MochiWeb and uses Postgres to store its data.

Interfacing with Ruby and Python

So you've been reading this book and thinking that Erlang sounds amazingly cool. You already have a web infrastructure in PHP, Python, or Ruby but you would love to be able to build some structure in Erlang. There are several ways you can do this. You could use something like RabbitMQ to couple different parts of an application with queues. You could also create a web service in Erlang and access it from another language, or send data over a socket. However, what would be really nice is being able to have native communications between Erlang and some other language.

This is actually fairly simple to do. As we know by now, Erlang processes can communicate over a wire protocol. When you send a message from process A to process B, all the data is serialized in some way and sent across to the other process to receive. Knowing that, you might think it would be pretty easy to create a package in another language that can speak that protocol and work with it, and of course you would be right. There are packages for Ruby and Python (and others) that can do that quite well. (Sending Erlang functions to other languages probably won't work.)

These interfaces can be used to mate a frontend in Python or Ruby to an Erlang backend or vice versa. They can also be used when porting some code to Erlang for testing. If you have a module that has been well tested in Ruby, for example, you could use QuickCheck to try a large number of test cases on both the Ruby and Erlang versions and make sure that both work correctly.

In order to have an Erlang node in some other language, there are a few actions that a package must be able to perform. It must be able to connect to an existing node and disconnect when done, and of course it must be able to send and receive messages from other nodes.

There is a module to interface PHP with Erlang called "mypeb" (*http://mypeb.googlecode.com*). However, I was unable to get it to compile.

Ruby

Erlang and Ruby can be interfaced with the `erlectricity` package that can be found at *http://code.google.com/p/erlectricity/source/browse/*. This package provides a Ruby interface that can interact with Erlang.

In Example C-1, which was taken from the `erlectricity` examples, after some initial setup there is a `receive` block created in Ruby. Here the syntax is distinctively Ruby, but the semantics directly parallel that of a receive block in Erlang.

The semantics of the `receive` block match those in Erlang. Here `receive` opens a block. The `receive` block uses the method `f.when` (line 8) to parallel the structure in Erlang quite nicely. Also note that the recursive structure of an Erlang loop is reproduced with the `g.receive_loop` method call.

To send a message from Ruby to Erlang you need the process ID. You would then use `f.send! :result, graph.to_blob`, which will send the message to the Erlang process. The Erlang process will receive a tuple of the form {`result, Blob`}.

Example C-1. gruff_provider.rb

```ruby
$:.unshift(File.dirname(__FILE__) + "/../../lib/")
require 'erlectricity'
require 'rubygems'
require 'gruff'

receive do |f|

  f.when(:plot, String, Symbol, String) do |name, style, font|
    graph = Gruff.const_get(style).new
    graph.title = name
    graph.font = font
    graph.legend_font_size = 10

    f.receive do |g|
      g.when(:data, Symbol, Array) do |name, points|
        graph.data name, points
        g.receive_loop
      end

      g.when(:labels, Erl.hash) do |label_data|
        graph.labels = label_data
        g.receive_loop
      end

      g.when(:end){ :ok }
    end
    f.send! :result, graph.to_blob
    f.receive_loop
  end

end
```

Python

You can interface Python with Erlang using **py_interface** (*http://www.lysator.liu.se/ ~tab/erlang/py_interface/*), which is a Python implementation of an Erlang node.[1] I checked the code out of Git and ran the script howto-make-a-new-version followed by configure and make, all of which seemed to work. My system is Ubuntu 11.10 and has Python version 2.7.2+ on it.

 In theory, you could create one node in Python and another in Ruby, and have them send messages back and forth with no Erlang in between. However, I am not sure this is actually a useful thing to do or a good idea.

While **py_interface** does not have a great manual, it does have a decent readme file and a good set of examples that can be used as a basis to explore how to do things. The bad thing is that the syntax of this module is not nearly as nice as that seen in Ruby.

Python is not really concurrent in the way that Erlang is, so the way things work is a bit different. Specifically, the Python API is single threaded and uses callbacks to handle messages from Erlang. The module also tries to map Erlang types onto Python as much as possible, and uses classes when it can't.

You can see a basic example of how to set up a Python node in Example C-2, which is taken from the **py_interface** examples. It imports **erl_node**, **erl_opts**, and **erl_even thandler** from the **py_interface** module. Then in the **main()** function it sets up a node with the function **erl_node.ErlNode(ownNodeName,** **erl_opts.ErlNo deOpts(cookie=cookie))**. It then publishes the node so that other processes can find it and registers the mailbox with **n.CreateMBox(__TestMBoxCallback)**. The callback **__TestMBoxCallback** is what actually responds to any incoming messages from Erlang. The rest of the function just sets up an event loop to wait for requests to come in.

Example C-2. Python example

```
#! /usr/bin/env python

import sys
import getopt

from py_interface import erl_node
from py_interface import erl_opts
from py_interface import erl_eventhandler

###
###
###
### TEST CODE
```

---

1. **py_interface** is licensed under the LGPL.

```
###
###

def __TestMBoxCallback(msg):
    print "msg=%s" % `msg`

n=None
m=None
def main(argv):
    try:
        opts, args = getopt.getopt(argv[1:], "?n:c:")
    except getopt.error, info:
        print info
        sys.exit(1)

    hostName    = "localhost"
    ownNodeName = "py_interface_test"
    cookie      = "cookie"

    for (optchar, optarg) in opts:
        if optchar == "-?":
            print "Usage: %s erlnode" % argv[0]
            sys.exit(1)
        elif optchar == "-c":
            cookie = optarg
        elif optchar == "-n":
            ownNodeName = optarg

    print "Creating node..."
    n = erl_node.ErlNode(ownNodeName, erl_opts.ErlNodeOpts(cookie=cookie))
    print "Publishing node..."
    n.Publish()
    print "Creating mbox..."
    m = n.CreateMBox(__TestMBoxCallback)
    print "Registering mbox as p..."
    m.RegisterName("p")

    print "Looping..."
    evhand = erl_eventhandler.GetEventHandler()
    evhand.Loop()


main(sys.argv)
```

Using Erlang with Emacs

For many Erlang developers, the editor of choice is Emacs. As a longtime Emacs user I have found there to be many reasons for this.

One feature of the Emacs Erlang mode is that you can compile a file by typing "C-c C-k", which will open Erlang in a shell and compile the buffer you are in. You can also copy and paste code from a buffer to an Erlang shell.

Being able to copy and paste code from a buffer to the Erlang REPL makes it very easy to explore solutions to a problem. The programmer can create a simple module and load it into Erlang with "C-c C-k", then create a bunch of test cases that are copied via standard Emacs editing to the shell to ensure that the code is working correctly. This does not replace formal testing, but supplements it when doing development.

In addition, the Erlang mode has a set of templates that can be used to create common structures. So if you need to work with the OTP gen_server pattern, you can generate the skeleton of that structure by opening up a new buffer and selecting the correct structure. The template for gen_server is shown in Example D-3 at the end of this chapter.

 Erlang comes with a very nice Erlang mode. You can find more details on it at *http://www.erlang.org/doc/apps/tools/erlang_mode_chapter .html*.

Distel

If you want to have a powerful interface between Emacs and Erlang, check out Distel mode. Distel (short for Distributed Emacs Lisp) extends Emacs Lisp to be able to speak to an Erlang node in a way very similar to Ruby or Python, as shown in Appendix C.

The Distel package can be found at *http://fresh.homeunix.net/~luke/distel/* and downloaded from there.

When starting up Distel, you need to tell it which node to talk to. It will prompt you for a node name, which can be in the form node@host or just node if it is local. Once you have given Distel a node name it will continue to use that node unless you prefix a command with C-u node-name.

Distel supports a number of features to make coding Erlang in Emacs easier. First of all, it supports completions of modules and functions by hitting M-?. It also allows you to load and evaluate Erlang code from the minibuffer. To load a module, use C-c C-d L and Distel will prompt you for the module name. Distel also features some pretty fancy refactoring tools.

In addition to tools, Distel also features some applications that can make working with Erlang easier. It features a process manager that will work from an Emacs buffer (C-c C-d l) and that allows you to find out all sorts of information about a process, including a backtrace and the contents of the process mailbox.

Distel will also allow you to interface Erlang's debugging facilities with Emacs, and will let you do all sorts of things to debug and profile Erlang code as it runs.

Finally, Distel will let you have a more powerful interactive session then the standard Erlang command line. Based on the Emacs Lisp *scratch* buffer, running an interactive session allows you to evaluate code directly from an editor buffer and see the results.

The Distel manual is only 11 pages long and can be found on the Distel web page. It's worth reading.

Flymake Mode

If you like using an IDE that highlights errors as you type, check out Flymake mode, which provides exactly that feature in Emacs. Flymake mode supports many languages, including Erlang.

In order to use Flymake, add the Emacs Lisp code in flymake.el (Example D-1) to your *.emacs* file. You may need to change the path to "flymake_emacs" to match the location of the file on your system.

Example D-1. flymake.el

```
(require 'flymake)
(defun flymake-erlang-init ()
  (let* ((temp-file (flymake-init-create-temp-buffer-copy
             'flymake-create-temp-inplace))
    (local-file (file-relative-name temp-file
        (file-name-directory buffer-file-name))))
   (list "~/bin/flymake_erlang" (list local-file))))

(add-to-list 'flymake-allowed-file-name-masks
        '("\\.erl\\'" flymake-erlang-init))
```

The Emacs Lisp calls the binary "flymake_erlang" to compile code as you type (Example D-2). This uses escript, which is a tool to write scripts in Erlang as you might do in Perl or Python. It does this by calling the function main/1 with a list of parameters.

Example D-2. flymake_erlang

```
#!/usr/bin/env escript
-export([main/1]).

main([File_Name]) ->
    compile:file(File_Name, [warn_obsolete_guard, warn_unused_import,
                             warn_shadow_vars, warn_export_vars,
                  strong_validation, report,
                  {i, "../include"}]).
```

Gen Server Template

Example D-3. gen_server.erl

```
%%%-------------------------------------------------------------------
%%% @author Zach Kessin <zkessin@gmail.com>
%%% @copyright (C) 2012, Zach Kessin
%%% @doc
%%%
%%% @end
%%% Created : 18 Jan 2012 by Zach Kessin <zkessin@gmail.com>
%%%-------------------------------------------------------------------
-module(gen_server).

-behaviour(gen_server).

%% API
-export([start_link/0]).

%% gen_server callbacks
-export([init/1, handle_call/3, handle_cast/2, handle_info/2,
     terminate/2, code_change/3]).

-define(SERVER, ?MODULE).

-record(state, {}).

%%%===================================================================
%%% API
%%%===================================================================

%%--------------------------------------------------------------------
%% @doc
%% Starts the server
%%
%% @spec start_link() -> {ok, Pid} | ignore | {error, Error}
%% @end
%%--------------------------------------------------------------------
```

```erlang
start_link() ->
    gen_server:start_link({local, ?SERVER}, ?MODULE, [], []).

%%%=====================================================================
%%% gen_server callbacks
%%%=====================================================================

%%---------------------------------------------------------------------
%% @private
%% @doc
%% Initializes the server
%%
%% @spec init(Args) -> {ok, State} |
%%                     {ok, State, Timeout} |
%%                     ignore |
%%                     {stop, Reason}
%% @end
%%---------------------------------------------------------------------
init([]) ->
    {ok, #state{}}.

%%---------------------------------------------------------------------
%% @private
%% @doc
%% Handling call messages
%%
%% @spec handle_call(Request, From, State) ->
%%                                   {reply, Reply, State} |
%%                                   {reply, Reply, State, Timeout} |
%%                                   {noreply, State} |
%%                                   {noreply, State, Timeout} |
%%                                   {stop, Reason, Reply, State} |
%%                                   {stop, Reason, State}
%% @end
%%---------------------------------------------------------------------
handle_call(_Request, _From, State) ->
    Reply = ok,
    {reply, Reply, State}.

%%---------------------------------------------------------------------
%% @private
%% @doc
%% Handling cast messages
%%
%% @spec handle_cast(Msg, State) -> {noreply, State} |
%%                                  {noreply, State, Timeout} |
%%                                  {stop, Reason, State}
%% @end
%%---------------------------------------------------------------------
handle_cast(_Msg, State) ->
    {noreply, State}.

%%---------------------------------------------------------------------
%% @private
%% @doc
```

```erlang
%% Handling all non call/cast messages
%%
%% @spec handle_info(Info, State) -> {noreply, State} |
%%                                   {noreply, State, Timeout} |
%%                                   {stop, Reason, State}
%% @end
%%--------------------------------------------------------------------
handle_info(_Info, State) ->
    {noreply, State}.


%%--------------------------------------------------------------------
%% @private
%% @doc
%% This function is called by a gen_server when it is about to
%% terminate. It should be the opposite of Module:init/1 and do any
%% necessary cleaning up. When it returns, the gen_server terminates
%% with Reason. The return value is ignored.
%%
%% @spec terminate(Reason, State) -> void()
%% @end
%%--------------------------------------------------------------------
terminate(_Reason, _State) ->
    ok.


%%--------------------------------------------------------------------
%% @private
%% @doc
%% Convert process state when code is changed
%%
%% @spec code_change(OldVsn, State, Extra) -> {ok, NewState}
%% @end
%%--------------------------------------------------------------------
code_change(_OldVsn, State, _Extra) ->
    {ok, State}.


%%%===================================================================
%%% Internal functions
%%%===================================================================
```

About the Author

Zachary Kessin has been working on developing interactive web applications since 1994. In the last few years, Zachary's focus has been on building complex applications in the browser with JavaScript, browser-based testing with Selenium, functional programming, and code generation.

Have it your way.

Get even more for your money.

Join the O'Reilly Community, and register the O'Reilly books you own. It's free, and you'll get:

- $4.99 ebook upgrade offer
- 40% upgrade offer on O'Reilly print books
- Membership discounts on books and events
- Free lifetime updates to ebooks and videos
- Multiple ebook formats, DRM FREE
- Participation in the O'Reilly community
- Newsletters
- Account management
- 100% Satisfaction Guarantee

Signing up is easy:

1. Go to: oreilly.com/go/register
2. Create an O'Reilly login.
3. Provide your address.
4. Register your books.

Note: English-language books only

To order books online:
oreilly.com/store

For questions about products or an order:
orders@oreilly.com

To sign up to get topic-specific email announcements and/or news about upcoming books, conferences, special offers, and new technologies:
elists@oreilly.com

For technical questions about book content:
booktech@oreilly.com

To submit new book proposals to our editors:
proposals@oreilly.com

O'Reilly books are available in multiple DRM-free ebook formats. For more information:
oreilly.com/ebooks

O'REILLY®

Spreading the knowledge of innovators | oreilly.com